Jesus' Parables Speak to Power and Greed

Westar Studies

The Westar Studies series offers distinctive scholarly publications on topics related to the field of Religious Studies. The studies seek to be multi-dimensional both in terms of the subject matter addressed and the perspective of the author. Westar Studies are not related to Westar seminars but offer scholars a deliberate space of free inquiry to engage both scholarly peers and the public.

Jesus' Parables Speak to Power and Greed

Confronting Climate Change Denial

Richard Q. Ford

Edited by Char Matejovsky

CASCADE *Books* • Eugene, Oregon

JESUS' PARABLES SPEAK TO POWER AND GREED
Confronting Climate Change Denial

Westar Studies

Copyright © 2022 Richard Q. Ford. All rights reserved. Except for brief quotations in critical publications or reviews, no part of this book may be reproduced in any manner without prior written permission from the publisher. Write: Permissions, Wipf and Stock Publishers, 199 W. 8th Ave., Suite 3, Eugene, OR 97401.

Cascade Books
An Imprint of Wipf and Stock Publishers
199 W. 8th Ave., Suite 3
Eugene, OR 97401

www.wipfandstock.com

PAPERBACK ISBN: 978-1-6667-3635-9
HARDCOVER ISBN: 978-1-6667-9451-9
EBOOK ISBN: 978-1-6667-9452-6

Cataloguing-in-Publication data:

Names: Ford, Richard Q., author. | Matejovsky, Char, editor.

Title: Jesus' parables speak to power and greed : Confronting climate change denial / Richard Q. Ford ; edited by Char Matejovsky.

Description: Eugene, OR: Cascade Books, 2021. | Westar Studies. | Includes bibliographical references.

Identifiers: ISBN 978-1-6667-3635-9 (paperback). | ISBN 978-1-6667-9451-9 (hardcover). | ISBN 978-1-6667-9452-6 (epub).

Subjects: LSCH: Jesus Christ—Parables. | Climate changes. | Global warming. | Church and the world. | Civilization—21st century.

Classification: BT375.3 F670 2022 (print). | BT375.3 (ebook).

VERSION NUMBER 082922

For my grandchildren's grandchildren,
who will surely ask of my generations,
"Why did you do so little when you could have done so much?"

The cover photograph is a sculpture by Robert Taplin of New Haven, Connecticut, titled *I Saw Shadows Coming (The Second Circle).* (Used with permission.) From a series titled *Everything Imagined is Real (After Dante),* Taplin uses Dante's verses to construct a parallel story.

From Dante v.106–111

We went in without a fight and I, who was eager to see what was within such a stronghold, as soon as we were inside, cast my eyes about and at every hand I saw a great plain full of torment and pain.

Contents

Introduction | ix

1. A Woman with Leaven, a Woman with a Jar, and a Man with a Sword | 1
2. A Widow and a Judge and the Wish for a Rescuing God | 5
3. Three Slaves and a Master (The Talents) and Fossil Fuel Executives | 23
4. Tenants and a Landlord | 44
5. A Slave and a Master (The Unforgiving Slave) | 58
6. A Manager and a Rich Man (The Dishonest Steward) | 69
7. The Poor and a Householder (The Great Banquet) | 80
8. Laborers and a Vineyard Owner (The Vineyard Workers) | 92
9. Jesus' Parable and the Genesis Stories of Two Sons and a Father | 101
10. A Samaritan and a Jew (The Parable of the Good Samaritan) | 118
11. Using These Parables to Explore Climate Denial | 128
12. Empathy | 141

Bibliography | 155

Introduction

Climate breakdown is real. It is irreversible. It is the most pressing, all-encompassing issue of the twenty-first century.[1] As the evidence mounts, fewer and fewer people the world over remain unaware of the scientific hypothesis that humans are responsible.[2] Yet many are in denial. They refuse to see what is in front of them. What informs the current refusal, by large segments of the population, to recognize the realities of climate breakdown?

The answer may be found in a narrative that is as old as human civilization, a story that goes back to the earliest human hierarchies. It tells of efforts to cling to power. When the few learned to control the fates of the many, they also mastered ways to justify that control. In service to the desire to possess more, they created stories of such conviction that they transformed what was once mere possibility into an inescapable imperative. These narratives enable and insist on the ongoing success of endless expansion.

In his day, Jesus confronted a narrative not unlike our own. He lived in an era when monetization of the economy rendered even more efficient the most efficient empire the world had yet seen. The worldview that subjugates the resources of the many to the control of the few was firmly entrenched in the Roman Empire of 2,000 years ago, as it is today in the American empire. Under the rubric "Pax Romana," Roman armies stripped everyone else of resources, sweeping a huge, one-way flow of land, goods, and slaves into the control of the elites.

---

1. The proposal to use the phrase "climate breakdown" to replace "climate change" was made by the British author and journalist George Monbiot in *The Guardian Weekly*.

2. An accessible presentation of the basic science is found in the Netflix TV series *Cosmos: A Spacetime Odyssey*, season 1, episode 12, narrated by Neil deGrasse Tyson, 2014.

Introduction

These elites created narratives—beginning with an account of the virgin birth of Caesar Augustus—that justified their right to exploitation. The central purpose of Roman imperial theology was to lock in the privilege of a few over the welfare of the many. "The gods have chosen Rome. The gods have determined that the Romans should be victorious with their military might. The gods have ordained Roman domination. This is not only the way things are; this is the way things are supposed to be." Thus, Caesar and the Roman aristocracy bestowed upon themselves the divine right to appropriate our shared resources.[3]

Jesus adopted a particular strategy in addressing the economic and social injustices that resulted. He told stories. Not treatises on societal dysfunction, but rather simple tales, called parables, that tell of two persons forced to rely on one another across widely differing economic and social positions. Of the longer parables that have survived, nine are thought by scholars to be authentic parables of the historical Jesus. In each, Jesus consistently employed the following plot devices: two characters, one possessing power and the other not, are placed in a situation of having to collaborate. Because of the differences in power, each perceives the other in a distorted way. As a result, collaboration disintegrates.

Jesus not only puts the economically dominant character in charge, he lets him pass judgment on his own behavior. In one way or another, these characters rationalize both their endless quests for the elusive gratifications of wealth and their distortions of protests by the powerless. Both themes call upon listeners to see what is not described: Nowhere is the deprivation for which the overlord is responsible addressed.

Jesus leaves entirely to his listeners the job of inferring what it is like to be exploited. He leaves to his listeners the work of seeing through the deceptions engineered by the dominant character. Listeners must wrestle with the ways in which each character's attitude towards the other makes sense. They must penetrate long histories of dominance and submission that precede the failed interactions in the story. These histories lead to misunderstandings that result in tragedy.

That task, the one Jesus assigned his listeners, resembles the challenge faced by those engulfed in the still widespread denial of climate change. Like the underlings in Jesus' stories, they must struggle on their own to perceive

---

3. When I pointed out to a Sunday school class that the Roman emperor, together with the Roman aristocracy, controlled probably 50 percent of the Roman Empire's wealth, a fourth-grader raised her hand and observed, "Oh! That's the way it is today. The 1 percent has all the money!"

Introduction

how they have been taken in and themselves become victims. Though the scientific facts of such imminent peril are increasingly acknowledged, even among deniers, the task of breaking through resistance to significant action remains formidable. To shift the paradigms of change, one must challenge economic certainties thousands of years in the making.

Jesus' parables are located precisely at the intersection of domination and submission. They interrogate listener propensity to hand authority over to an overlord—to allow that authority not only to define what is going on but simultaneously to dismiss the point of view of the underling. Jesus has us straddle a fissure characteristic of all societies, but one that has become particularly dangerous for our own.

When these stories are seen as complex commentaries on cultures of dominance and submission, they spring to life in our contemporary world. Clearly, Jesus was not confronting the unprecedented realities of global warming. Nonetheless, his parables consistently engage what is perhaps the central issue in climate denial, namely the way humans, in order to dominate others, deceive themselves. His exceedingly brief narratives offer exceptional insights into the range of human motivations to "not see." Even the gospel editors minimized his invitation to wrestle with the misperceptions occurring between superiors and inferiors. Instead of understanding each character as equally involved in a conflict with the other, they transformed the powerful character into an allegorical figure for God. The resulting prospect of a rescuing God obscured the realities of human conflict.

If we accept that we are not going to be released from the consequences of climate change through some kind of adaptive intervention from above, then we must work to find terms to express the seeming contradiction, "How can a God who does not intervene be with us?" These enduring parables provide a forum for such work.

All of Jesus' longer narratives leave a great deal unsaid. They are replete with carefully crafted gaps, which the listener must fill to make sense of the whole. They become what we make of them. For this reason, his parables have no right or wrong interpretations. How we fill in the gaps tells us less about the stories than about ourselves. What these stories do, brilliantly, is allow us more readily to understand what we have chosen to see and what not to see.

By converting the parables' ambiguous invitation into an expectation that God will intervene, we overlook the myriad ways these narratives respect the role humans have to play. Do we choose to emphasize how God will intervene to bring about growth and harmony? Or, when confronted with the corruption inherent in human hierarchy, do we recognize how we ourselves are called upon to intervene? The essence of this second response is captured in an aphorism attributed to St. Augustine: "Without God, we cannot; without us, God will not."

I

A Woman with Leaven, a Woman with a Jar, and a Man with a Sword

We start this book with three very brief parables, almost certainly authentic to the historical Jesus,[1] and placed side by side in the Gospel of Thomas.

A Woman with Leaven

Jesus [said],
(a) The Father's imperial rule is like [a] woman
(b) who took a little leaven, [hid] it in dough,
(c) and made it into large loaves of bread.

A Woman with a Jar

Jesus said,
(a) The Father's imperial rule is like a woman
    who was carrying a [jar] full of meal.
(b) While she was walking along [a] distant road,
    the handle of the jar broke, and the meal spilled

---

1. One possible criterion indicating which of the longer parables may be attributed to the historical Jesus is the presence of *sustained* tension between its two major participants.

behind her [along] the road. She didn't know it;
she hadn't noticed a problem.
(c) When she reached her house, she put the jar down
and discovered it was empty.

A Man with a Sword

Jesus said,
(a) The Father's imperial rule is like a person
who wanted to kill someone powerful.
(b) While still at home he drew his sword and thrust it
into the wall to find out whether his hand would go in.
(c) Then he killed the powerful one.
(Thomas 96–98 Scholars Version)

~

The parable of the leaven underscores the efficacy of collaborating within the limits of nature. Its image of yeast immersed in flour evokes the ever-widening patterns of interaction characteristic of natural growth—of seed enclosed in soil and semen fertilizing an egg. Both in its evolutionary history and in the mother's womb, the beginning swelling into life is imperceptible. ("The seed would sprout and grow, he does not know how" [Mark 4:27].) From ancient times to the present day, this process yields enormous satisfaction and endless mystery.

The parable of the jar, with its suggestion of miscarriage, delivers the shock of unexpected moments of disaster—of malfunction in the natural order, but not of malfeasance. In the leaven, the plot line is utterly predictable. In the jar what should have been commonplace gets traumatically disrupted. Neither of these two stories gives human initiative pride of place. Both privilege natural forces.

When considering the three stories as a whole, what stands out is how radically the parable of the man with a sword differs from the first two. It breaks with their depiction of the natural order. The stories progress from collaboration with the natural order (leaven), to anonymous disaster within the natural order (jar), to humans operating outside the natural order (sword). Instead of describing what the natural order does for or to humans, the third parable focuses on what humans do to each other. It replaces the dominance of the natural order with the dominance of human decision-making. Put in terms of climate breakdown, the first parable may be said to describe the benefit of operating within the known boundaries of climate, and the second to depict the disruptive power of climate. Against that backdrop of the natural order acting predictably or erratically, the third stands out by referencing humans acting to transform climate. It thus embodies the endless human conceit that coercion can escape retaliation.

Unlike the leaven, the outcome in the sword is unpredictable. Because the man gains his authority through violence, justified or not, that authority is perennially vulnerable to overthrow by greater violence. And just as the one man shoves his sword into the body of another, so humans inject deadly amounts of carbon dioxide into the atmosphere. Because we gain our position by violence, not collaboration, we too will be subject to retaliation by greater violence.

If the yeast can be seen to represent natural fruition, and the jar to represent natural disaster, the sword can represent deliberate human attacks on human bodies. Here is one human body, integrating untold layers of complexity, now suddenly disemboweling, deadening, and draining another of all possibility. This instant of violence stands in utter contrast to the eons of evolution required for the first mitosis of the first cell—an event surely equal in magnitude to that first moment in which the universe itself was born. Moving from the expansion of the big bang to the mitosis of a cell to the birth of a self-awareness capable of imagining the murder of a rival, we arrive at a central question: How can the self-determining human live in concert with the eons of developing life contained within the natural order? The answer can be found in Jesus' manner of living. The only way to be kingly is to be subject to. In being "subject to," Jesus exemplified what the natural order requires of humans if they are to thrive.

Though a man's sword can be readily interpreted as sexual, the challenges of today's world require us to look beyond the image of a male thrusting a sword into a female body. The image of the "sword" must be expanded to represent an exponentially larger means of destruction. Here "bodies" must be understood to include political bodies, national bodies, and world bodies. The critical involvement of individuals controls the fate of millions. We have reached a moment in evolutionary time when a few persons are capable not only of destroying each other but of endangering all humanity. We face the reality of destruction that is not only caused, but *planned,* by humans. The newly powerful man wants to penetrate, exploit, and destroy the natural order, and the body of Mother Earth herself. Here we see the face of willful human destruction of the very source of life.

This present reflection is from a contemporary perspective. It leaves open the question of how an ancient might have imagined the contest between emerging life and sudden death. Nonetheless, the sequential placement of these three parables enables both ancients and moderns to perceive the contrast among the natural emergence in the leaven, the perturbations of nature in the jar, and the unnatural ambition in the sword. The murderer intends, in an instant, to disrupt and then transform the progression of eons. He will upset the rhythms of the natural order, whether beneficent or tragic, with his willingness to use violence to effect change. He will disrupt the natural order and bend it to his will. He neither consults others nor doubts his design—only his courage. He knows the right way to go. He will not see that his intervention will provoke counter-interventions. He believes he can escape retaliation. He is the epitome of the interventionist. He is the embodiment of the self-deceived. As he strides forward, believing he can survive and succeed, he becomes a masterful representation of the strong man denying the coming retaliation of climate breakdown.

2

A Widow and a Judge and the Wish for a Rescuing God

Among Jesus' longer narrative parables, the most condensed and most complex is that of a widow and a judge. It reads as follows:

The Situation

> In a certain city there was a judge
> who neither feared God
> nor had respect for people.

Scene 1

> In that city there was a widow
> who kept coming to him and saying,
> "Grant me justice against my opponent."

Scene 2

> For a while he refused,

Jesus' Parables Speak to Power and Greed

Scene 3

> but later he said to himself,
> "Though I have no fear of God
> and no respect for anyone,
> yet because this widow keeps bothering me,
> I will grant her justice,
> so that she may not wear me out
> by continually coming."
>
> Luke 18:2b–5 (NRSV)

INTRODUCTION

The concept of Christian religious literacy encompasses two very different but interactive domains, one of historical reconstruction and the other of modern response. For the response to be appropriate, the reconstruction must first be adequate. Likewise, unless it is refreshed by modern response, historical reconstruction will atrophy and be relegated to the ivory towers of academia. In that case many of us reading this book would simply close its pages.

This chapter focuses on the three sentences that comprise the outline of an enigmatic and complex parable of Jesus, that of the unjust judge. To our advantage the narrative calls less for an understanding of time-bound social and economic conventions than for an appreciation of the illusions required for the exercise of power. Illusions, unlike conventions, are timeless. Across centuries, continents, and civilizations, they regularly infect humans who reach for the pinnacles of power. They are as disconcerting today as they were when the character of the judge was first conceived.

Many listeners are deeply troubled by the ways in which this parable seemingly champions a combination of absolute power and absolute self-delusion. The parable firmly discounts the age-old hope that "our God will save us." Whatever vindication the widow receives comes about for all the wrong reasons. Any hope that justice will prevail is eradicated. Instead, the narrative focuses on the judge's mocking question. He asks, in effect, "Where is your God?"

This seeming breakdown of law is so appalling that listeners, beginning with Luke, find it impossible to tolerate. Luke wrote:

A Widow and a Judge and the Wish for a Rescuing God

> And the Lord said, "Listen to what the unjust judge says. And will not God grant justice to his chosen ones who cry to him day and night? Will he delay long in helping them? I tell you he will quickly grant justice to them." (Luke 18:6–8)

The parable virtually compels listeners to introduce a deity who intervenes. However, to do so, listeners must fly in the face of Jesus' insistent exclusion of that solution. They must confront the fact that *nowhere* in the story does Jesus provide any hint of God's intervention. Even Luke, when attempting to rectify this omission, dares not tamper with the parable's construction. Left standing on its own, that structure seems to exclude all possibility for justice.

Nonetheless, listeners must respect the boundaries of the story. They must not fall prey to Luke's urgent editorial intervention, one that releases the narrative's tension and altogether vitiates Jesus' challenging invitation.

For those who remain within the boundaries of verses 2b–5, the task of creating coherence throws up questions such as: What forces drive this intimate, utterly impersonal conflict so squarely situated within a massive imbalance of power? What motivates the widow's extraordinarily dangerous behavior? What provokes the judge's implacable resistance? Why doesn't she just give up? Why doesn't he just give in? Why, in fact, does he ultimately give in? Only after thoughtful consideration can we turn to the contemporary query that will be addressed later in this chapter: How does our understanding of this ancient struggle inform our experience of the present impasse we so desperately confront today?

THE JUDGE

It is important to recognize the extraordinary degree to which the judge must exclude data. His commitment to ignorance is not born of indifference; rather, it is a highly motivated strategy of pivotal significance. His determination to prevent other perspectives from penetrating his awareness forms an armor plate that repels any and all external influences. He imagines he owes nothing to tradition or culture, to family or colleagues. No hero compels his allegiance, no peer his admiration, no law his loyalty, no alternative perspective his attention.

This vacating of the influence of others, this ironclad refusal to entertain outside points of view, is critical to the judge's functioning. His ability to maintain the delusion of control centers on his capacity not to know.

Jesus' Parables Speak to Power and Greed

The only way he can dominate is by being completely right. Compromise is unthinkable; opponents must either submit or retreat. At the expense of consulting no one, he has achieved a complete lack of doubt. By dint of his flawed internal structure, he can muscle in and take others over—but only to a limited extent. He has no real interest in competing among the powerful. He is instead obsessed with humiliating the powerless.

Not only does the judge fail to provide anything from within that will sustain the widow's initiative, but he openly boasts of his ability to ignore, and thereby render useless, any appeal to law she might make. The judge's self-deception is staggering. A supposed student of law, he will disregard the Torah, the foundation of Jewish culture that has endured across millennia, despite repeated efforts from multiple conquering nations to undermine it. He will pit himself against an entire people and their sustained determination to remain loyal to their covenant with their God.

The extent of the judge's investment in a single perspective is astounding. Without the evidence of current events, we might find it difficult to believe such a figure could exist, much less be selected for high office. The judge eviscerates every opposing position. He neither respects people nor fears God. The wholesale rejection of other points of view is the price he must pay to safeguard his illusion of control. No one, no external principle, has purchase on his determination to be the one who defines the rules. Any hierarchy of what might matter most is missing. This obliteration of distinctions is crucial; it renders useless any appeal to reason.

The judge represents those people who seek power not for its own sake, but in order to forcibly overcome the ways in which they themselves were dominated. His longstanding campaign to control others is almost certainly a reaction to an earlier experience of being controlled. Lost in the distant past is how he was once humiliated the way he now humiliates others. His passion serves but one purpose, namely, to transform those who once shamed him into those he can now shame. His task requires political astuteness, endless duplicity, and an enormous capacity to betray. Dismissing responsibility, empathy, and concern, his behavior is shaped not by external realities but by internal imperatives. His ability to dominate present representatives of those who once oppressed him affords him extreme satisfaction. He feels that he has at last succeeded in overcoming his mortification.

Thus, the judge is captivated by motives other than greed. He is drawn less by wealth than he is driven by the hope that he can overcome his past trauma. Money and position are indeed necessary as the means of control and as the source of protection from challenges to that control, but the basic motivating force in the whole enterprise is a determination never to be humiliated again. Put another way, he seeks to gain emotional security that cannot be wrested from him. "I will be honored and elevated—and no one will be able to touch me." However, in order to achieve such illusory control, one must jettison basic human insights; for instance, that human happiness is found not in taking more but in sharing what you have. Power disengages the internal brake on greed. When that brake no longer holds, the resulting desire for more leads to a never-ending desire for more.

Although the widow may challenge the judge, she cannot transform him. He is unreachable because he is in the grip of a conviction, tragically validated by his near-term success, that the only way to overcome control is through counter-control. The judge is vulnerable to defiance on one front only, namely, his certainty that he is in control. To support that certitude, he must interact only with those he is confident he can dominate. He picks off the outliers. Because his ambition is premised on the idea that you can *force* someone to do something, he cannot escape the impulse to inflict revenge. Put another way, he cannot escape repeating his past. What is completely preempted is any influence able to counter his determination to do to them (persons in the present) what they (completely different persons in the past) did to him. Ironically, all the judge succeeds in doing is inflicting on others what he so hated when it was forced on him. In his efforts to achieve "Never again!" he has managed merely to impose "Forever the same!"

THE WIDOW

In his rush to shift the balance of power, Luke may be missing the potency in the widow's persistence. Like David with the giant Goliath, she has found the chink in the judge's armor. As with any schoolyard bully, no matter how large the difference in strength between persecutor and victim, the former cannot tolerate persistence. Put another way, he cannot manage not being able to instill fear. By continuing to challenge the judge, she reawakens the age-old terror driving his present determination, namely, his fear of those persons in his past whom he could not dominate. It becomes a duel of perceptions. While he acts as if he might destroy the widow, all he wants is to reassure himself that he can humiliate her. Instead of groveling, she responds without fear. In what appears to observers and probably to herself as involving immense risk, the widow calls his bluff. He in turn cannot abide this reawakening of the very real danger imposed by his long-gone adversaries.

Here we discover a truly remarkable contrast. In the judge's world, the widow barely exists. While she may have some purchase on him as an object, she has no purchase on him as a person. Their relationship is the most vacuous, the most lacking in substance, of any in the parable corpus. Yet, through her persistence she comes closer than any other parable subordinate to tearing his world apart. When he finally realizes the shape of her resolution, like an insect caught in a bright light, he abruptly scurries away. Ironically, the judge's boast of being able to dominate millennia of Jewish self-determination is rendered vacuous by his inability to dominate a single, vulnerable woman. The widow's stubborn refusal to be intimidated punctures his grandiosity. With his fantasies frustrated, and with a transparently inadequate excuse, he flees the field. "*Parturiunt montes, nascetur ridiculus mus*—Mountains are in labor, a ridiculous mouse will be brought forth."[1]

While the widow is determined to have the judge act on her behalf, the goal of her quest is ambiguous. Is she seeking justice or vengeance? The Greek verb *ekdikeō* can mean either "to procure justice for someone" or "to avenge someone." The uncertainty about her goal may, in fact, accurately represent what for her has become a growing ambivalence. She has arrived at a critical crossroads.

She has badgered him for a very long time. "Grant me justice against my opponent." "Feel what I feel." She has been thoroughly blocked from access to law. Now the judge, for all the wrong reasons, is showing signs of weakening. She recognizes in herself a certain effectiveness. With that growing sense of power comes a desire to coerce. At this juncture she is at risk of abandoning her quest for fairness in favor of misusing power. Here she is caught at the very moment that she is tempted to turn from seeking justice and to imposing revenge, at which point she would shift from being oppressed to becoming an oppressor. "I want to use this judge to *make* my opponent feel the same way he made me feel." After having been powerless for so long, it is at this moment of uncertain power that religious people are drawn to fantasizing how they might harness their God to punish their persecutors.

---

1. Horace, *Ars Poetica* line 137.

Given her own limited success, the widow must work to maintain her quest for justice and not let herself retreat into the dead-end of coercing revenge. Jesus even has the voice of the widow echo that of a compromised God. "I will get satisfaction from My foes; I will wreak vengeance on My enemies" (Isa 1:24). Here is a grappling with the very divine violence in the Old Testament that is destined to permeate the New. How does one negotiate an escalating resentment at being abused without succumbing to a thirst for vengeance? The question is no longer whether God will intervene; the question becomes, "How can any intervention transform the endless revival of violence in which even the divine can be implicated?"

Here the listener must weigh the internal motives that support the widow's persistence. Is the desire for revenge sufficient to sustain the ongoing risk she is taking in confronting this powerful man's refusal to recognize her claim, much less enact justice? Is the woman simply beating her head against a wall? Or might she be doing something else?

RAPTURE THEOLOGY

When religious people feel their backs are against the wall, when they perceive the powerful of the world to be in widespread control, they can be tempted to imagine a God who will inflict never-ending punishment and reestablish long-lost justice. Both impose change from without. Neither acknowledges that true change comes only from collaboration. It is astonishing to discover how these two incompatible resolutions exist side-by-side and without apparent conflict in the New Testament book of Revelation. There readers will find support for these conflicting positions. The author maintains the contradictions by attributing them to the divine. God intervenes to bless some and punish others. It is important to observe how profoundly the present parable rejects *both* of these resolutions. Even under the enormous weight of lawlessness on the part of the Roman occupiers and the Jewish aristocracy, Jesus refuses to entertain *any* intervention from his God.

Jesus thus eschews the temptation embraced by John of Patmos, the author of the book of Revelation. John promotes a rescuing God to accomplish what for him is a definitive, endlessly sustainable conclusion. He would have his God include some and exclude others. For John, the intervention of his God is utterly powerful, utterly good, and utterly violent.

Jesus' Parables Speak to Power and Greed

Revelation's vision places greater emphasis on retribution than on restoration. In contrast with the characters who represent redemption, those set for destruction are depicted in more color, with more depth and more impact. "Babylon," "the Great Whore," and "the Beast," all tropes for the Roman Empire, are vividly described, disgraced, and decimated. Divine intervention is premised on splitting humanity into "good" and "bad." Revelation's theme is of an end time when wrong is put right, and proponents of evil are not only banished but given over to everlasting suffering.

A widely popular, contemporary fundamentalist Christian point of view, which might be termed "rapture theology," relies substantially on the book of Revelation. The word "rapture" itself does not appear in the Bible. It comes from the Latin word *rapare*, which means to "seize," "snatch," or "take away." Based initially on a passage from Paul (1 Thess 4:13–17), its fundamental idea is that, at the end time when Christ returns to earth, the "good" will be transported to a "new earth." Everyone else will be left behind to suffer in a corrupted, damaged, and deteriorating world. (This basic idea has informed the immensely popular *Left Behind* series of books by Tim LaHaye and Jerry B. Jenkins.)

When contrasting Jesus' parable with John's vision, it is hard to imagine any greater disparity. The parable describes a widow barely able to withstand the strength of the oppressive judge. The book of Revelation insists on an assured, violent intervention that is complete, victorious, and permanent. In the parable, the widow, with difficulty and at great risk, pokes at the eye of the judge.[2] In Revelation, "the angel swung his sickle over the earth and gathered the vintage of the earth, and he threw it into the great wine press of the wrath of God. And . . . blood flowed from the wine press, as high as a horse's bridle" (Rev 14:19–20).

The seemingly fatal drawback of rapture theology—namely, its perpetual failure to come to fruition—does not impact its survival. After every disappointment, its adherents merely reassess and reset the rescue date to some future time. Over and again, this theology regains its robustness because so many want it to be true. Hot emotion trumps cold facts.

For those who adopt it, this theology is irresistible. It is hard to imagine a better remedy for working-class conservative Christians in their struggle to counteract the humiliating success of modern liberals. The oppressed

---

2. The Greek verb *hupōpiadzō*, translated as "wear out" ("I will grant her justice, so that she may not wear me out by continually coming") literally means "to strike under the eye." The image comes from boxing.

finally realize their desire to oppress the oppressors. All that had been lacking was access to power.

Because the book of Revelation originated within the cauldron of religious persecution, revenge is disguised as rectitude and punishment as the will of God. On the one hand, the redeemed will instantly be relieved of all the adverse consequences of sharing one earth. On the other, God will abandon the oppressors to their fate. While in rapture theology the seeming emphasis is on the graciousness of God, even more obvious is how the elites will be defeated. Such theology simply reverses elite domination. "You thought you had access to all the power. But we have access to all of God. Our ability to crush you in the same way you have crushed us far outweighs any satisfaction we might gain from the arduous work of reconciliation." At the cost of imposing the irrational, this theology demolishes the intolerable.

However, what the book of Revelation promotes as radical change in fact represents a depressing continuity. The zero-sum game is the same; only the goalposts are switched. "You deprived us and escaped into privilege. Now Christ is going to take us to heaven, and you are going to be left behind. Instead of you being on top, we're going to be on top. And you, my dear friends, are going to be on the bottom. We will escape. Unfortunately, you will not."

This theology provokes scorn among progressive Christians. The challenge for religious liberals is to overcome their temptation to continue dividing Christians into "bad" and "good." They should, rather, work to develop respect for the reasons behind this conservative theology.

For those who have lost much of their own world, rapture theology offers recourse to a far better one. It promises people who have long been dominated by elites the satisfaction of seeing those elites destroyed. When approaching such a belief system, progressive Christians need to tread carefully. Those of us who have been economically successful, who have not been subject to coercion, are tempted to look down on those who have been economically deprived and who have come to believe they can win only through coercion. Having been held down for so long, they understandably look for theologies which promise pushback. (Three major exceptions to this pattern are found in the extraordinary nonviolent leadership of the civil rights movements in India, the United States, and South Africa.)

While we may very well sniff their arrogance, can we also get a whiff of our own? Are we essentially any different? Are we prepared to denigrate their dream while tenaciously holding on to our own? Think of the book of Revelation as winning the lottery. Do not take away that dream without offering something to replace it. And do not dismiss it without at least considering the possibility that nothing will replace it. Does satisfaction at the promise of the rapture differ in any essential way from satisfaction at the prospect of economic success?

THE PARABLES AND THE WISH FOR A RESCUING GOD

Humans resist the work of enabling God's desire. They have difficulty embodying the conditions for human collaboration or embracing the limits in the natural order. Thus, parable-listeners are tempted to place their hopes in the dominant character as representing God's preparedness to intervene. For example, in the parable of the wicked tenants, they discover a God who sacrifices the life of his beloved son; in that of the talents, a God who rewards those who are faithful; in that of the vineyard workers, one who is generous to those who come last; and in that of the unforgiving slave, a God who forgives an astounding debt. These powerful God-figures are able to correct the muddled destructiveness found in human affairs. They promise divine rescue from the consequences of human decisions.

This interpretation entails difficulties. First, because we so want to find rescue embodied in the parable's dominant character, we choose to ignore the many indications that the strong man is in fact devoted merely to his own aggrandizement. Second, by depending on the strong man, we fail to see that it is *our* job to resolve the dilemmas that exist between a superior and a subordinate.

Among the most attractive aspects of power is its seeming capacity to compel outcomes. In religious terms, we first impute this imagined power to God. We then believe ourselves to be capable of persuading this God to intervene. We want comfort, not accountability; control, not hard work. When a psychotherapist hears a patient say, "You are the best therapist ever," the therapist recognizes the difficulty. There is a large demand hidden in such praise: "I will idealize you, and then *you* will do all the work." Much of religious discourse is susceptible to efforts to make similar bargains. We prefer not to be held responsible for what we do. We want our God to fix things. Whether we imagine ourselves inhabiting earthly miracles or neighboring planets, we are still prone to smuggle in a fundamental conviction that we can achieve positive change only through coercion; if not ours, then God's.

The parable of a judge and a widow lampoons that presumption. It does not present a figure whom the listener would wish to have intervene. Rather it presents someone who is all intervention, who does to the world whatever he pleases. How close is he to the God of the book of Revelation? How much does that God render unnecessary our need to contribute to outcomes? To what degree is he the embodiment of the God we hope for?

In an environment of self-generated threat, we seek stories of rescue. We tend to define such rescues as love. Thus, we are caught in an inevitable, longstanding conflict between necessary dependency and needed autonomy. In the earliest stages of human development, love means "We will do it for you." Later on, love goes in the opposite direction, "Difficult as it is for us, we will *not* do it for you." For parents of adolescents, these two tendencies are at odds with one another. The familiar sense of being in control when providing for our children gives way to an unfamiliar loss of control when having to trust them. In turn, like adolescent children, we struggle all of our religious lives with a similar ambivalence about what kind of God we want.

The parable of the unjust judge explores a radical investment in ignoring limits. A form of this commitment is represented by those Christians who are enthralled by the idea that a "new earth awaits them after death." The central feature of their new earth is the absence of limits. Death is abolished; life is everlasting. Consider the blasphemy in this objective. It constitutes a critique of the God of creation. This theology declares the present creation, the present universe, the present natural order—all of which are governed by entropy and death—to be not good. In imagining a world without death, we humans aspire to correct God's error. We would revive the endless human quest for "more" while dismissing the one reality that motivates us to accept limits. We would deprive ourselves of the discoveries that come with a life lived within the boundaries of death.

The goal of otherworldliness rips apart a unity central to ancient Hebrew sensibility, "God saw all that he had made, and found it very good" (Gen 1:31). Similarly, it eviscerates the central appeal of the Lord's Prayer, "Thy will be done on earth," that is, on *this* earth, the only earth there is. It eradicates the whole of humanity's struggle to achieve God's desire in the world in which we live. In a new earthly paradise, we would once again, with exhausting imprecision, neglect the essential conditions of being human, namely, embracing limits and thereby being interdependent. We would, instead, keep alive the ambition to gain access to "more," thus restoring the conditions for an endless seeking of more.

The matter goes deeper. We are not only seeking religious privilege. Hidden inside these theological formulations is the quest for economic advantage. In Jesus' time, the greed of elites drove some 5 percent of people at the bottom—the "expendables"—to an early death. Something like that reality has ever been the case. It still is. Because of the maldistribution of wealth and the fact of limited resources, any remaining excess is available only to a few—and an important segment of that group wants even more. For them to possess more, others must be dispossessed. Justification for such taking requires the splitting of humanity into possessors and expendables. This disruption of the interdependent unity of the natural world is necessary to maintain economic control.

A particular example stands out. Protestants in the southern United States abandoned the biblical investment in human equality and divided humanity into insiders and outsiders. They shifted the emphasis from social justice to a concern for individual salvation in order to obviate equality between Christian slave and Christian slavemaster, a move necessary to maintain what was an essential economic perversion. Betraying that unity insured the continuing economic advantages of slavery.[3]

When interpreting parables, even liberals who malign conservatives for upholding an interventionist God may find themselves supporting a God who intervenes. Listeners can be enticed to assign the dominant parable character the role of a rescuing God. They can perceive this superior as able to fix what is wrong. Neither conservatives nor liberals, however, have been able to explain how those dominant figures can right wrongs by excluding. The parables are skillfully constructed to leave room for others who wish to imitate the ways these players disguise, both from themselves and others, the harmfulness of their dominance. They do so not only by

---

3. I owe this observation to David Greer, personal communication. The twin admonitions, "Slaves obey your earthly masters with fear and trembling, in singleness of heart, as you obey Christ" (Eph 6:5) and "Slaves obey your earthly masters wholeheartedly . . . fearing the Lord" (Col 3:22) cannot be by Paul because they are in contradiction to what Paul writes in his letter to Philemon. They are by later revisionists seeking to bring the radical Paul back in line with established Roman norms. (The two former letters are generally dated some decades after Paul's death.) Writing to Philemon, Paul is diplomatic but adamant. For Paul, a Christian master cannot own a Christian slave. They are brothers. (See Crossan, *God and Empire*, 160–65.)

excluding the humanity of their victims but also by denying they are the ones who have made things unworkable in the first place.

Here we come upon a stunning realization. Jesus' parables are pessimistic. All of these brief stories address but cannot resolve unrelieved structural deficits. A persistent widow is vindicated, but the overarching lawlessness is left untouched. Although a disabled Jew is given a chance to heal, the surrounding prejudice remains an open wound. And while a vineyard owner is momentarily generous, the longstanding maldistribution of wealth persists. Likewise, in the other parables, the conclusions are mired in dysfunction: in that of the prodigal son, undiminished shame; in that of the great banquet, an unsustainable future; in that of the talents, irresolvable recrimination; in that of the dishonest steward, an unsustainable future; in that of the unforgiving slave, torture; and in that of the wicked tenants, murder.

We ignore these defects. We prefer religious narratives that both permit us to continue destroying limits *and* provide us with a God who will deliver us from the consequences. It is one thing to wish for an intervening God when we see social compacts broken, for example, when our government deliberately separates children from their immigrant mothers. It is quite another to invoke an intervening God to help us escape the aftermaths of our own efforts to breach nature's limits.

INTERWEAVING THE PARABLE WITH MODERN DENIAL

Because we are able to break the limits that have heretofore preserved the natural order and thereby induced climate change, humanity is poised to inhabit an unforeseen version of the earth as we know it. We are, as yet, only in the late mid-phase of that experience. However, if we fail to employ our ability to anticipate, we and our descendants will find ourselves sharing the repercussions already afflicting our poorer neighbors. Though we may not, as yet, have reached some irreversible threshold, it will soon be too late for us to change course. Then we will have no choice but to endure the world we have initiated.

Instead of engaging God's desire—which could be understood as the natural world's need for us to embrace the limits of the earth—we resist recognizing that the natural order cannot adapt to the greed pressed on it by humans. True, for a time nature will appear to absorb our burgeoning load of carbon, but that absorption will inevitably break down. Climate denial appears as one, albeit crucial, version of our widespread refusal to foresee the consequences. Never before has the capacity to anticipate been imparted with such import to a single species. That ability affords us the chance to redeem our future. But, while we have the facts, we are not sufficiently anxious. We refuse to acknowledge the catastrophe of climate breakdown. Thus, we squander the opportunity inherent in our accomplishment.

Why should "God" restore the natural order that we are intent on destroying? Why would we expect the natural order to overcome our destruction of it? Imagine, for instance, that unnatural interventions were to take place, that the carbon suddenly vanished from the atmosphere. Would humanity not revert to its familiar maldistribution of wealth? Would not the privileged resume occupying all of the atmospheric commons? How can these self-defeating tendencies ever be conquered? Overcoming climate denial does not simply mean stopping what we are doing. It involves learning to do things differently.

In contemporary life, the rescuing God of Christianity has morphed into the rescuing Magician of Technology. We believe that somehow technology will intervene to save us. In 2014, Naomi Klein published an immensely important book entitled *This Changes Everything: Capitalism vs. the Climate*. In a chapter entitled "No Messiahs," she describes

> what may be our culture's most intoxicating narrative: the belief that technology is going to save us from the effects of our actions . . . [A]midst ever more sinister levels of inequality, most of us have come to realize that the oligarchs who were minted by the era of deregulation and mass privatization are not, in fact, going to use their vast wealth to save the world on our behalf. Yet our faith in techno wizardry persists, embedded inside the superhero narrative that at the very last minute our best and brightest are going to save us from disaster. This is the great promise of geoengineering and it remains our culture's most powerful form of magical thinking.[4]

In his parable Jesus appears to pin his God between two unacceptable alternatives: (1) God does not hear, is absent, is indifferent (as portrayed by the figure of the judge), or (2) God is powerless, helpless, unable to realize justice (as portrayed by the figure of the widow). The parable is so structured that a third alternative cries out to be included: God will indeed

---

4. Klein, *This Changes Everything*, 255.

intervene to establish justice. Luke writes, "And will not God grant justice to his chosen ones who cry out to him day and night?" (Luke 18:7). He adds this commentary in an urgent effort to break up the parable's carefully crafted, insistent refusal to admit such intervention. The parable itself ends at 18:5. Nowhere within its compact boundaries is there any hint of divine rescue. There is, however, a fourth alternative.

HOW THE WIDOW BREAKS THROUGH

In an era of climate breakdown, belief in an intervening God—now transformed into confidence in the ever-promising Magician of Technology—is among the most dangerous of fantasies. Based on the empathic work required to engage the parable and embodied in the faithfulness of Jesus, this section draws on a very different reading for insights into how we might respond to the awesome, daunting, urgent problem of climate breakdown.

The parable encompasses, with particular clarity, the conflict between human and divine desire. Essential to the judge's desire is taking control, rejecting, and demanding. Essential to God's desire is allowing, tolerating, and not intervening. Here we confront a powerful human determination to ignore God's wishes, set side-by-side with what appears to be an appalling lack of interest on the part of the divine. Paradoxically, immersing listeners into the pessimism of his parables may reflect Jesus' confidence that his God inhabits the very center of that pessimism. As we enter the parable's darkness, God accompanies us.

Here we may find evidence of how Jesus understood the presence of his God in the midst of imperial domination. Here we may glimpse Jesus' inner resources when confronting the entrenched powers of Jerusalem and Rome. Here we can ponder how Jesus' response can inform our own sense of hopelessness when confronting the awesome dimensions of climate change.

Jesus' reliance on listener response to his parables may in fact be evidence that he trusts their capacity to be faithful, just as he has been faithful. We are "saved" not by "faith in Christ" but by emulating Jesus' faithfulness as he responds to the faithfulness of God. Just as being faithful to the longing of God forms an indestructible bond between human and divine, so also faithfulness to the ways of the natural order will bring humans and nature together in a lasting bond, regardless of the outcome.

Jesus' Parables Speak to Power and Greed

The refusal of those in control to recognize the experience of those who are not sits at the heart of climate denial. Likewise, the judge's full-blown resistance to recognizing the experience of the widow occupies the center of the parable. With unrelenting vigor, the judge denies himself the slightest spark of empathy. When dismissing the widow, he indulges in a savage attack on fellow-feeling: "I have no fear of God nor respect for anyone." He is willing to empty out the widow as well as himself rather than accept that he might be in the wrong. That perspective is painfully widespread, both then and now. Under its tyrannical pressure the longing for outside intervention intensifies.

While it may not promise success, empathy—the ability to feel what the other person feels—is the most effective tool available to prevent our imminent collapse into warring tribes. That ability to appreciate the experience of another is precisely what the judge is trying to kill, and what the widow is struggling to keep alive. The widow does not try to overpower the judge. Crucially, she does not attempt to wrestle with him on his terms. Neither does she move away from him. Rather she moves toward him. She insists that he acknowledge how she feels.

The judge attributes the widow's breakthrough to the most banal of reasons: she makes him feel uncomfortable. That is his internal reality. But her internal reality—as she repeatedly confronts his seeming strength from a position of seeming weakness—is the same as that of anyone of us who chooses to struggle against climate denial. The task is discouraging in the extreme. She is pitting herself against the most implacable of opponents. The judge represents those who have no interest in arguments from science. He is unreachable. The widow must struggle again and again with his smoothly rationalized façade. Without appealing to divine intervention, she perseveres. What keeps her going?

Of the factors that drive the widow's persistence, two stand out: the quest for justice or, failing that, the thirst for revenge. The listener must weigh these disparate motives. Is the desire for revenge sufficient to sustain her efforts given the danger she provokes when confronting the judge's refusal to enact justice? Or is she perhaps aiming at something other than the judge, something outside him? What if she is determined that justice should not be perverted by the mere willfulness of one troubled person? Could her confidence in the justice embedded in the Torah and essential to the God of Israel be sustaining her tenacity? What if, in today's lingo, she feels drawn into the force field central to the maturing universe?

A Widow and a Judge and the Wish for a Rescuing God

The widow *is mobile*. Despite the constricting reality of her world, she reaches out, seeking and trying. In contrast the judge's world is so self-sufficient that it renders him functionally inert. He will not allow anyone to become sufficiently close for him to believe that that someone might respect him. He can only manage to cringe and withdraw. And he commands too much power ever to acknowledge his fearfulness.

The parable invites the listener to join with the widow, who in turn may be seen as joining with Jesus in faithfulness to his God. In the face of the massive oppression of Rome and Jerusalem, in spite of the opposition arrayed against him, Jesus responds faithfully to the divine desire. So does this widow. She embodies Jesus' own courageous faithfulness to the just ways of the God of Israel. "God," the essential creative force within the universe, stands with *her* rather than with the judge—not because she is better than her oppressor, but because she fits with the way things need to be.

The heroism of the widow and that of Jesus are similar. Despite the overwhelming power of her opponent, *she moves forward*. If she can maintain her balance, if she can resist the temptation to transform her quest for justice into a quest for revenge, she, like Jesus, will have a powerful effect in an overpowering world. Whatever happens, she is with God and God is with her. Luke is half right when he reflects on the tension in God when engaging human injustice. In light of the parable, he might better have written, "And will not God *hear and suffer with and yearn for* his chosen ones who cry out to him day and night?" The entire struggle between letting go and trusting, on the one hand, or grabbing on and controlling, on the other, is captured in this story. Everything depends on identifying the nature of the presence of God. We do not have to overcome in order to affirm that presence, but we do have to affirm that presence in order to keep on striving to overcome.

Absence of God's intervention does not mean absence of God's presence. God's refusal to intervene in fact reveals a presence that combines profound concern with immense respect. The work of emulating that presence spreads out across the universe. In these difficult times it has become *the* central resource for maintaining both our integrity and our ability to fight back.

Herein lies the foundation for a persistent if seemingly hopeless involvement. We can reach out to each other because, by standing with God, we perceive God's presence in one another. Empathy is reciprocal. To be given, it must first be received. To possess it, we must first feel we are being felt. God's longing is not subdued by the judge's overwhelming power. Like Jesus, the widow is sustained by faithfulness to the justice inherent in the God of Israel. She becomes someone with whom the God of the universe stands.

Success is not discovered in simply being successful. Success is found in being *with* God. The God of Jesus, the God of this remarkable parable of darkness, is present with the widow—and with us. S/he suffers and yearns with the widow on behalf of all of humanity. While s/he will not intervene, s/he is completely *with* everyone who seeks to be with "God."

3

Three Slaves and a Master (The Talents) and Fossil Fuel Executives

The Situation

For it is as if a man, going on a journey, summoned his slaves.[1]

Scene I

and entrusted his property to them; to one he gave five talents, to another two, to another one, to each according to his ability. Then he went away.

---

1. For centuries nearly every English translation of the two slave parables in this book has rendered the Greek word *doulos* inaccurately as "servant." (This bias is less evident when *doulos* is encountered in the Pauline Epistles, where the word often receives its proper meaning of "slave.") "Servant" obscures the term's essential significance for these parables, namely, that one human being retains complete control over the life choices of another. Such has been the strength of this bias that it took the translators of the august Revised Standard Version until 1989, in the New Revised Standard Version, to render the word *doulos* correctly as "slave."

Jesus' Parables Speak to Power and Greed

Scene II

The one who had received the five talents went off at once and traded[2] with them, and made five more talents. In the same way, the one who had the two talents made two more talents. But the one who had received the one talent went off and dug a hole in the ground and hid his master's money.

Scene III

After a long time the master of those slaves came and settled accounts with them. Then the one who had received the five talents came forward, bringing five more talents, saying "Master, you handed over to me five talents; see, I have made five more talents." His master said to him, "Well done, good and trustworthy slave; you have been trustworthy in a few things, I will put you in charge of many things." . . . And the one with the two talents also came forward saying, "Master, you handed over to me two talents; see, I have made two more talents." His master said to him, "Well done, good and trustworthy slave; you have been trustworthy in a few things. I will put you in charge of many things." . . .

Then the one who had received the one talent also came forward, saying, "Master, I knew that you were a harsh man, reaping where you did not sow; and gathering where you did not scatter seed, so I was afraid, and I went and hid your talent in the ground. Here you have what is yours." But his master replied, "You wicked and lazy slave! You knew, did you, that I reap where I did not sow, and gather where I did not scatter? Then you ought to have invested my money with the bankers, and on my return I would have received what was my own with interest. So take the talent from him, and give it to the one with the ten talents."

(Matt 25:14–30 NRSV)

---

2. "Traded" is a too precise, and therefore misleading, translation of the Greek verb *ergadzomai*, which means "to work" or "to be active."

Three Slaves and a Master (The Talents) and Fossil Fuel Executives

INTRODUCTION[3]

Jesus' longer parables are characterized by the breakdown of shared goals. They begin with two parties—a superior and a subordinate—each wanting something from the other. However, this tentative moment of mutuality quickly devolves into unbridgeable differences. A momentary collaboration around shared goals becomes one in which the underling must serve only the interests of the overlord. The superior's insistence that the subordinate submit to *his* goals—against which the subordinate rebels—upsets an already fragile balance.

Misunderstandings necessarily follow. Since power enforces silence, a lack of communication between the superior and the subordinate is inevitable. "I have the power. I can refuse to absorb your legitimate protest. I can cut the wire from the engine to the oil gauge." (That I might have to suffer down the road for this choice is wonderfully obscured.) The inability of the superior to recognize and describe what is really going on enables the ensuing violence. Violent consequences are thus not accidental or inadvertent, they are structural and inevitable.

Of all the characters appearing in Jesus' parables, the talentmaster and the unjust judge are the most powerful, crass, and resistant to change. The talent master, however, is a more suitable model for modern oligarchs than is the judge, who is driven to overcome an earlier humiliation. Like modern oligarchs, the talentmaster is specifically addicted to accumulating more. Both he and his modern counterparts believe they have the power, and the untrammeled right, to hurt others. Likewise, in modern America, the pervasive casting of doubt on the well-established findings of climate science owes in large part to the expanding rule of the very rich.

THE TALENTMASTER

Across the history of this parable's interpretation, the description by the third slave of the master's way of being—embraced and repeated by the master himself—has most often not been heard for what it is. Even though Jesus takes pains to emphasize what is in fact going on, we persist in misunderstanding. Twice we are told that this man goes through life "reaping"

---

3. For the basic orientation of this chapter, I am indebted to the seminal work of two authors: Ngũgĩ wa Thiong'o, *Devil on the Cross*, and William Herzog's "Vulnerability of the Whistle-blower," chapter 9 in *Parables as Subversive Speech*.

where he did not "sow." Though present-day readers may have difficulty grasping the subtleties of the ways in which one went about making large sums of money in southern Galilee in the early part of the first century,[4] Jesus leaves no doubt about the nature of the master's enterprise.

Steeped as we are in the mores of modern capitalism, Western listeners regularly fail to see how the peasants in Jesus' original audiences would have perceived this man's mode of operation. He is a criminal. He is stealing the land and labor of others. He first chokes off peasant protest, then raises a single, powerful voice to assert his own entitlement. Having claimed the right to take from others, he continues misleading listeners right down through the ages.

In a 1993 article on this parable, Richard L. Rohrbaugh pointed out the reality of limits in such closed economies. "There simply is not enough of anything to go around or any way to increase the size of the pie. . . . What this means is . . . a larger share for one automatically means a smaller share for someone else." Thus "a master getting one thousand percent on his money [according to Luke 19:16] would be viewed as greedy to the core."[5] Christoph Kähler is more explicit: he sees the master as "inhumanly hard," "a blood-sucker," "an oppressor," and "a thief."[6]

"I reap where I do not sow" means "I take where I do not contribute." No external constraint, no inner conscience, no sense of limit interferes with this man's aggrandizing of wealth and power. "I take where I do not

---

4. For a description of the aggrandizing strategies of the agrarian aristocracy of Jesus' time, see Ford, *Parables of Jesus*, 31–35.

5. Rohrbaugh, "Peasant Reading," 33, 35.

6. Kähler, *Jesu Gleichnesse als Poesie und Therapie*, 171, 172, 173. A large amount of work appears necessary, often in collaboration with people who are poor and dispossessed, to rediscover what was once a given. For two of the places where this insight first broke into American awareness, see Fortna, "Reading Jesus' Parable of the Talents."

Here Fortna describes a prison inmate who, when describing the master, suddenly realizes, "He exploitin' me, man!" (214). See also Cardenal, *Gospel in Solentiname,* where Nicaraguan *campesinos* tentatively perceive the third slave's courage: "The guy didn't get much, one talent; he didn't cooperate . . . He was conscientious, because he didn't have the strength to exploit his brothers and sisters" (quoted in Fortna, "Reading Jesus' Parable of the Talents," 215n8).

In his magnificent chapter, "Vulnerability of the Whistle-blower," William Herzog built on these earlier insights to create a comprehensive interpretation. Referring to the work of Cardenal, Herzog writes that of "all the contemporary commentators on the parable, the peasants of Solentiname were the ones to intuit the economic system that underlies the parable [as] . . . 'a very ugly example . . . of exploitation'" (Herzog, *Parables as Subversive Speech,* 160–61).

contribute because I *can*—and no one can stop me." One could not find a more accurate summation of Roman imperial ideology. This boast likewise echoes the position of modern oligarchs. No regulatory agency, no governmental law can prevent their rapaciousness. They can take advantage of others with impunity. The resulting massive distortion in the distribution of wealth makes it easy to see the ultimate consequence: eventually there will be more nonsowing reapers than sowing ones. Like the talentmaster, the oligarchs cannot see that they are in the process of consuming their own base.

Arnold Toynbee, the British historian famous for his efforts to compare civilizations across all known history, has this to say about the Assyrian Empire:

> The disaster in which the Assyrian military power met its end in 614–610 B.C. was one of the completest yet known to history. It involved not only the destruction of the Assyrian war-machine but also the extinction of the Assyrian state and the extermination of the Assyrian people.[7]

Toynbee explains this disaster as follows:

> [In the Babylonic Society] . . . Assyria was a march whose special function was to defend not only herself but the rest of the world of which she formed a part from . . . predatory [outsiders] . . . [W]hile the march is stimulated in so far as it responds successfully to its proper challenge of resisting external pressure, the interior is relieved of pressure and set free to face other challenges and accomplish other tasks. This division of labour breaks down if the frontiersmen turn the arms which they have learnt to use against the outsider into a means of fulfilling ambitions at the expense of the interior members of their own society. . . . The aberration of the march which turns against the interior is, of its very nature, disastrous for the society as a whole, but for the marchman himself it is suicidal. His action is like that of a sword-arm that plunges the blade it wields into the body of which it is a member.[8]

While the judge distorts an entire world within his own imagination, the talentmaster perverts a structure existing within his closed agricultural economy. While the judge is more unreachable, the master is more immediately vicious. Both behaviors beg for answers: How is their wanton

---

7. Toynbee, *Study of History*, 338.
8. Toynbee, *Study of History*, 343.

sadism gratifying? Are they better off for the pleasures gained by means of their control? Does ruining the lives of others make them happier? Most importantly, how can the talentmaster not realize he is undermining the very structures that support his dominance?

One means of access to the talentmaster's self-deception may be through our own obliviousness. How is it we cannot see the malevolence in this despicable man? How is it we so freely turn over to him the authority to tell us what is actually going on? Is it because we wish to imagine that the people in charge are on our side? That they are like us and want to do well by us? That they will not let us down?

This parable is as close as Jesus comes to describing the Roman Empire. His narrative encapsulates the ways in which imperial ambitions undermine the norms of society. What is novel in today's world are not the distortions, which continue unchanged down to the present, but the scale of damage inflicted. The talentmaster's greed pales by comparison to the magnitude of avarice straining global limits and threatening all humanity.

THE SLAVES

The slaves in this parable occupy the "upper" levels of ancient slavery. The first two slaves gain access to power at the cost of their own integrity. In the same way they have been dominated, they dominate the economic well-being of the peasants. Unlike the third slave, they do not risk their position. Because it emulates the ways of their master, their behavior is rewarded.

The choices of the first two slaves can be seen as an apt metaphor for membership in modern fossil fuel corporations. Just as the first two slaves orient themselves to their master's desire, so corporate members embrace the ways in which corporate cultures navigate the boundary between obligatory profit-making and human well-being. The orientation of high-level fossil fuel executives is to their CEOs. The orientation of the CEOs is to their stockholders. These loyalties pressure them to deny nature's limits. For them climate denial is just one more version of a larger, longstanding set of justifications, employed by many but not all corporations, for promoting profit over the common good.

The first two slaves fit well within the illusion of well-being promulgated by their master. The clear-eyed third slave refuses to go along with such wishful thinking. He knows his master is not taking care of those subject to him. He knows his lord is not creating a workable world of sharing.

Three Slaves and a Master (The Talents) and Fossil Fuel Executives

THE THIRD SLAVE

The talentmaster's certainty, as he boasts of his criminal enterprise, suggests how completely he is convinced of his right to exploit. It leads him to misdiagnose as incompetence what is in fact resistance on the part of the third slave. That he understands the problem to be stupidity is evidenced by his gratuitous efforts to teach his slave what he should have done. At the same time, by cloaking his resistance as incompetence, the third slave is able to deceive his master. Here there is considerable irony. This slavemaster, who lives off the labor of others, condemns his slave for being "wicked and lazy." He judges that his slave's refusal to make money by hurting other people, and thus imitating his master, renders him unfit to belong to his inner circle. He embodies the same arrogance, prevalent today, which demands subordinates gain wealth at the expense of others.

The third slave in this narrative has been particularly misunderstood. He is the only one of the three to reject the master's mode of exploitation. By refusing to maximize profits at the expense of peasants, by refusing to imitate his lord, this slave is putting his life at risk. To keep his integrity and still stay alive, he acts as did many slaves in the United States. He disguises resistance as incompetence.[9] While his fellow slaves take cover in the safety of conforming, he works hard at doing nothing. On his lord's return, he suffers the expected disdain and ostracism.

It takes work to comprehend the irony embedded in this narrative. The third slave, who appears to be weak and vacillating, in fact defeats the self-centered purposes of a particularly powerful man. Nowhere in the run-up to the denouement does he betray his intentions. Things are not as they seem. The slave's intent is carefully masked. Listeners are caught denying (overlooking) his extraordinary bravery. Here is someone who acts without regard for his own safety or self-advancement; he calibrates his behavior to how well it benefits others.

It is worth considering how the figure of the third slave might be autobiographical. It may be evidence of how Jesus saw himself. He is every bit as vulnerable as the third slave. Through the person of the talentmaster, Jesus is confronting powers as cruel and self-centered as the Roman Empire and the Jewish aristocracy.

What is it that impedes our understanding? Is it simply that we concede authority to those who confidently claim it? Do we tend not to feel the

---

9. See, for example, Osofsky, *Puttin' on Ole Massa*.

pain of those whose voices are not heard? Are we misled by the third slave's seeming cowardice?

Here we must pause, step back, and look carefully at how Jesus has constructed this parable. We are amazed to discover that he has slanted his narrative in favor of our *not seeing*. His parable functions in exactly the same way as did the aristocracy of his day. (It also describes perfectly the behavior of today's oligarchs.) It elevates the voice of the oppressor. It supports the definitions of the aristocrat and permits no other perspective. It obliterates the voice of the oppressed and renders the underclass invisible. It admires the master's final crushing of dissent. It gives authority to those who see only what they want to see.

With breathtaking artistry, Jesus has adopted the elitist perspective. How better to draw us into identifying with the very persons who oppress us? How better to leave entirely to us the work of extracting ourselves from this skein of misperceptions? How better to equip us with ways of grappling with our own propensities not to see?

Listeners must decide whether Matthew 25:30, "As for this worthless slave, throw him into the outer darkness," is part of Jesus' original parable or is Matthew's addition. Matthew believes that this judgment, which in fact is determined by the master's greed, is accurate. He thereby understands the slave's remarkable courage as cowardice, a conclusion listeners have accepted down through the ages. Matthew clearly discovers in this narrative an allegory for the last judgment. Listeners persuaded by his understanding will have difficulty integrating the master's exploitation of others. If they wish to perceive the talentmaster as a God-figure, then they must also attribute criminality to God.

INTERWEAVING THE PARABLE WITH MODERN DENIAL

The figure of the talentmaster, created 2,000 years ago, lives on in the present. The modern oil executive is similarly dedicated to the pursuit of more and equally able to justify why this pursuit should come at the expense of others. That the talentmaster is ensnared by his perspective can be seen in his outburst, "You wicked and lazy slave! You knew, did you, that I reap where I did not sow . . . ? Then you ought to have . . ." (Matt 25:26, 27 NRSV). His entitlement pervades his self-consciousness. He is not slowed by regard for others. He lives in a world where no institutions exist to curb his rapaciousness. He exhibits the same absence of guilt as do his masters in Rome. For him, exploitation is simply a fact of life. He cannot conceive that anyone, certainly not this cowardly slave, would dare intervene on behalf of mere peasants. The idea of anyone feeling concern for such people is beyond his imagining.

To achieve power over others and over the environment requires the systematic erosion of empathy. The oligarchs[10] of today, who have chosen to pursue extraordinary wealth, have long abandoned any consideration for those they deprive. For both the talentmaster and his modern colleague, the inability to feel guilt eviscerates any predilection they might have had to change. They must eschew such feelings to be able to function. Their very success insulates them from fellow-feeling. They use their enormous wealth to put themselves beyond the reach of those they have harmed.

The denial of climate change unites both oligarchs and blue-collar workers: the former seeks to gain economic power and the latter to overcome economic deprivation. Both groups, for different reasons, feel they do not have enough.

THE "MORE" OF THE OLIGARCHS

Much of secular belief is invested in two visions of the future: (1) confidence in the ongoing success of economic expansion, undeterred by planetary limit, and (2) faith that any encountered limit can be overcome by technological innovation. Absent is any recognition of the age-old propensity of a few powerful individuals to dominate the resources of everyone else. These few are driven by an endless, insatiable quest for *more*.

Almost a thousand years ago, around 1080 CE, a Benedictine abbot, later to become Archbishop of Canterbury and even later to be canonized, wrote a thirty-page book entitled *De Casu Diaboli*, or *On the Devil's Fall*. In

---

10. The term "oligarch" is used here to capture the contemporary concentration of both enormous wealth and enormous political power in the hands of a very few. The charity Oxfam issued a report in January of 2018 showing that "42 people hold as much wealth as the 3.7 billion who make up the poorest half of the world's population." It added that "82% of the global wealth generated in 2017 went to the wealthiest 1%" (Lawson and Martin, "Commitment to Reducing Inequality Index 2018." To cement its analogue with men like the talentmaster, the term "oligarch" is restricted to those who have not only crossed the boundary into taking from others without obligation but who manifest no meaningful concern for the harm they are inflicting.

Jesus' Parables Speak to Power and Greed

it he crafted one of the most persuasive analyses of the nature of evil that can be found in the Western corpus.

In a nutshell, St. Anselm thought that the essence of evil was wanting "more." He further believed that the character of this "more" could never be specified. "More" is incapable of definition because it represents a human goal incapable of fulfillment. It is not something that exists separately in reality. "More" has two dysfunctional, distinguishing characteristics: (1) If you achieve it you will be satisfied. (Therefore, if you are not satisfied, you must revert to seeking even more.) (2) Achieving "more" is always premised on compelling others to submit. (Thus, the goal of achieving "more" obviates the need to win trust.) This combination of expectation and control is remarkably resilient; it has dominated all of human history. Those who agree to it live with an uncertain certainty about their position.

Trying to gain "more" through coercion can never succeed. Like a mirage, it is always out of reach. An investment in coercion, which indeed seems to promise success, ironically undermines the very conditions for success. Coercion eliminates any chance to experience the gratification of trusting others and the pleasure of having "enough"—the fundamental rewards promised by the elusive achievement of "more."

Possession of any tantalizing piece of "more" pulls its possessors away from the gratification provided by others and pushes them to pursue the "more" beyond the horizon. It jettisons any concept of enough and eliminates any chance of trust. Though the gratification of "more" seems always to be within reach, it becomes everlastingly elusive.[11] Ultimately, the option "to grab on to is to lose" is the only option in play. Its precious alternative, "to let go of is to have," remains forever out of reach.

Like telling lies, compelling others to submit will snowball. Once you have embarked on such a course, you must continue escalating. You cannot turn back. Admit to one lie, openly regret one arm-twisting, and the whole enterprise begins to unravel. As that prospect is unacceptable, you must keep tightening your control in pursuit of the elusive "more." The self-deception that reaching one's goal is possible becomes the basis of one's very existence.

Because more has no end point, arriving at a place where enough is enough is always beyond reach. Here is the "black hole" at the center of oligarchic desire: When is enough enough? A billion dollars? Ten billion dollars? A trillion? Simple greed is insufficient to account for the tenacity

---

11. For the content of these two paragraphs, see Mathewes, "On Self-Deception."

of this drive. One understanding would see the underlying motivation to be a chronically unsatisfied effort to compel respect. "The more money I have, the more I can *make* you respect me." This formulation, although appearing watertight, excises an essential component: respect is won, not compelled. That compelled respect is a false coin is evidenced by its never being enough. The goal of securing true respect remains endlessly elusive, locking its adherents into forever seeking "more."

The higher one climbs the echelons of respect, the more one's audience shrinks, until the only opinion worth having is from those with whom one is most competitive, namely, fellow billionaires. In the end, however, that which is pursued is merely an illusion: coercion evokes only the appearance of respect. Ever lying in wait for its possessor is a resentment born of envy. Here in semi-awareness, is the certainty of loss that every aspiring "king of the mountain" must carry inside throughout the arduous ascent to the summit.

The limitless greed of the powerful requires them to insist that there is no limit to the capacity of the natural order. "More" must always be available. Their insatiable desire makes that assertion nonnegotiable. Accepting that there are limits, a requirement communicated by climate science and enforced by global physics, effectively undermines belief systems built on coercing respect. This system cannot tolerate the immovable limits reported by science or enforced by reality. It simply ignores them. It insists that science is arrogantly out of step and denies human-caused climate breakdown. The messenger must be shot.

THE "MORE" OF THE UNDERCLASS

We turn to another insistent vision of limitless resource, that nurtured by deprived white, lower-middle-class workers in the United States. Here the fact that resources are limited thwarts their insistence on regaining lost access to the American Dream. The reality that American jobs in manufacturing and mining, for example, have been irretrievably lost due to limits on resources, is unpalatable. Unfortunately, their understandable hopes are kept alive by the empty promises of politicians.

The oligarchs have long known how to co-opt politicians in their attack on "big government," thereby eluding, in a single brilliant maneuver, both recrimination and regulation. To the advantage of the oligarchs and the disadvantage of everyone else, their political representatives subvert governmental regulation, destroy environmental protections, and deny climate breakdown.

For their part, politicians satisfy their supporters with the appearance of success. They do not do the demanding work of formulating new solutions. Rather, they tear down what already exists and tout it as a new beginning. Through such seemingly effective destruction, and at no cost to themselves, they gratify those who have long had to endure humiliation. The equation seems to be, "Since you have destroyed what we want, our side will destroy what you want."

Although both upper-class oligarchs and lower-class workers share the outrage at the restraining limit, only oligarchs benefit. While skilled politicians give voice to the resentment of their working-class supporters, hidden is how the aspirations of those same supporters are eviscerated by the greed of the oligarchs. The oligarchs' promise to restore self-respect is erected on a foundation of disrespect. Their manipulation of the working class is carefully orchestrated not to expose the lack of interest by political "leaders" in rescuing their supporters.

INTERNATIONAL CORPORATIONS

Limitless entitlement among the oligarchs fits well within the structural entitlements accumulated by modern international corporations. Given the approaching, irreversible tipping points imposed by climate change, the evolving power of international corporations is now at the center of humanity's struggle for well-being. Time is of the essence. While the destructiveness of climate breakdown will unfold gradually across centuries, any opportunity to slow its effects is confined to the decades immediately ahead. Yet corporations work steadily to abolish federal regulation constraining climate change. No overarching corporate governance oversees their functioning.

While the federal government is tasked with responsibility for citizen welfare, corporations do not shoulder that responsibility. Rather, the basic duty of corporate executives is to secure "more" for their stockholders. No executive can survive who does not service this requirement. Having progressively neutralized governmental regulation, corporations are becoming a law unto themselves. The place of humans inside them is problematic. Are they in control of, or are they controlled by, the corporate ethos? Based on their hierarchical, nondemocratic structure, corporations have been able to create an economic culture which renders "normal" the siphoning of money from the less wealthy to the wealthier. Their very success creates an unstoppable momentum in favor of corporate control over democratic institutions. The ability of an elected government to intervene, to regulate, is increasingly undermined by oligarchic control. Their lobbyists become our legislators. According to *Fortune*, in 2021, "corporate pretax profits surged 25% year over year to $2.81 trillion . . . when taxes are factored in, corporate profit increases . . . soared 37% year over year."[12]

Because corporations are undemocratic, fossil fuel leaders are insulated from significant opposition. Their authority derives from their predecessors, not from any electorate. In the absence of governmental regulation, few mechanisms exist to challenge leadership distortions. Because they are structured as top-down hierarchies, those below have little incentive to risk criticizing decisions of those above. Rewards and punishments are governed merely by the short-term demands of stockholders. When confronting the long-term dangers of climate change, corporate leaders escape any significant counterpressure from within their own organizations.

The conformity demanded by modern corporations is analogous to that demanded by ancient slavery. Like the slaves in Jesus' parable, if you are a rising executive in a financial institution or corporation, and if their practices happen to hurt people, you are to put profit ahead of people. Those outside the corporate system, just as those outside the constraints of ancient slavery, often underestimate the dangers facing whistleblowers who must still function inside a pressure-cooker of stringently enforced demands to adapt.

THE UNIQUE POSITION OF FOSSIL FUEL EXECUTIVES

Fossil fuel corporations also reap where they did not sow. The concentrated forms of carbon that they mine and sell took millions of years to develop. These corporations have gained their enormous wealth by taking possession of a commodity they did not create. Nor have they reimbursed the rest of the world for the costs of its consumption. They have instead used their profits to increase governmental subsidies for their enterprise and to decrease governmental regulation of their profits. In the meantime, "black gold" has morphed into "black death."

12. Daniel, "U.S. Companies Post Their Biggest Profit Growth in Decades," paras. 2, 3.

Jesus' Parables Speak to Power and Greed

Corporate purpose is structured so that priorities within fossil fuel corporations have become indistinguishable from the extraordinary dangers of mining those fuels. Under the guise of "fiduciary responsibility," they not only refuse to take responsibility for the effects of their pollution, but they have also persuaded governments to subsidize it.[13]

That these executives have made choices for profits and against people is amply documented. By the early 1980s, scientists from Exxon (later ExxonMobil) developed state-of-the-art research demonstrating that CO_2 emissions would cause global warming and unacceptable damage to the environment. According to Bill McKibben, "management believed the findings—as the *Los Angeles Times* reported, companies like Exxon and Shell began redesigning drill rigs and pipelines to cope with the sea-level rise and tundra thaw."[14]

Executives then set the scientists to work looking for solutions. When, after great effort, the scientists could discover no cost-effective ways to mitigate the coming damage, Exxon's leadership reversed course. Money for research was cut off and redirected to a long-term campaign to evoke public doubt about the science they had heretofore supported. McKibben writes, "In 1997, just as the Kyoto climate treaty was being negotiated, Exxon CEO Lee Raymond told the World Petroleum Congress meeting in Beijing, 'It is highly unlikely that the temperature in the middle of the next century will be significantly affected whether policies are enacted now or 20 years from now.'"[15]

Similarly, a 1988 Shell Oil confidential report, recently discovered by Dutch journalist Jelmer Mommers of *DeCorrespondent*, reveals that by 1988 Shell was not only aware of the threats posed by climate change, but acknowledged internally its own role in creating the conditions for a warming world.

The report states that climate impacts could include "significant changes in sea level, ocean currents, precipitation patterns, regional temperature and weather." It also states that changes would impact "the human environment, future living standards and food supplies, and could have major social, economic and political consequences." Shell's authors detail additional, specific impacts including the abandonment of cities and countries in low-lying areas (e.g., Bangladesh) and coral reef destruction.

---

13. See Doukas, "Talk is Cheap."
14. McKibben, "Winning Slowly Is the Same as Losing," para. 6.
15. McKibben, "Winning Slowly Is the Same as Losing," para. 1.

It concluded that these environmental and socioeconomic changes may be the "greatest in human history."[16] Nonetheless, in the following decade, despite claiming to support the 1997 Kyoto Protocol and stating that they "wanted to take the precautionary route on climate change, [Shell Oil's] ... principal solutions to CO_2 emission reductions involve[d] consuming and extracting more oil and gas."[17]

The CEOs at both ExxonMobil and Shell knew but deliberately chose "not to know." Their mantra became "scientific uncertainty." Relying on science's normative inability to arrive at absolute certainty, their public relations campaign sought to misinterpret high probabilities as signifying the absence of persuasive data. "[Y]ear after year, the industry used the review process of the Intergovernmental Panel on Climate Change to stress 'uncertainty,' which became Big Oil's byword." A famous Exxon internal memo declared: "Victory will be achieved when average citizens 'understand' (recognize) uncertainties in climate science" and "when uncertainty becomes part of the 'conventional wisdom.'" When corporate leadership found that it could not overcome the challenge to its profits posed by the laws of physics, it turned to one it could, namely, manipulating public opinion. Insiders would know, but no one would tell the world.[18]

One of the handful of people who are major contributors to climate breakdown is Rex Tillerson, formerly CEO of ExxonMobil and later, for a time, U.S. Secretary of State. Tillerson is this generation's Dick Cheney. Both are powerful oil men going after the big prize. Former Vice President Cheney evinced no interest in negotiation. He pursued his goal by gaining political power and then using military force. In order to get to what he wanted, he had to break apart the political structures protecting it. Ironically, his quest to secure the self-aggrandizing Iraq Oil Law foundered in an Iraqi parliament made so dysfunctional by U.S. policy that it could not be manipulated. And any progress made in the subsequent decade was obviated by the Islamic State's takeover of many Iraqi oil fields.[19]

Tillerson, by contrast, pursues the big prize by combining access to massive amounts money with exceptional abilities as a negotiator. Environmentalist Bill McKibben reports that in 2012 Tillerson told a New York audience that global warming is real, but he dismissed it as an "engineering

16. Climatefiles, "1988 Shell Confidential Report," paras. 7 and 8.
17. Climatefiles, "1998 Report," para. 4.
18. Material for this paragraph was drawn from Banerjee et al., "Exxon," para. 7.
19. See Watts, "We Have 12 Years."

problem" that has "engineering solutions." Such as? "Changes to weather patterns that move crop-production areas around—we'll adapt to that... The fear factor that people want to throw out there to say, 'We just have to stop this,' I do not accept," Tillerson said. Of course not—if he did accept it, he'd have to leave his reserves in the ground. Which would cost him money. It's not an engineering problem, it's a greed problem.[20] Tillerson's casual words, "We'll adapt," betray a staggering arrogance. How will the entire world adapt to out-of-control sea levels, hurricanes, fires, drought, disease, famine, and institutional collapse? His words betray a shocking disregard for human rights. They represent nothing more than a hollow promise of rescue used to camouflage relentless self-interest.

Tillerson offers no evidence that his corporation has engaged in a careful analysis of the costs of adaptation, nor of the economic disruption, political upheaval, and psychological trauma involved in such a massive transition. The carelessness of his comments reveals that he is looking merely for excuses to continue business as usual. At the time he spoke those words, he clearly knew that decades earlier Exxon's scientists had tried and failed to come up with proposals able significantly to mitigate the coming damage. He was present when his corporation's entire strategy for confronting climate change shifted from problem-solving to cover-up.

With "we'll adapt," Tillerson reveals that he understands the effects of climate breakdown but chooses to disregard their costs. He is in fact saying, "Let us continue burning carbon, destroying the environment, and making huge amounts of money, and somebody else—certainly not us—will come along and fix all the damage we have caused." Notice the false equation: "*We* do not have to respect limits because *someone else* will fix whatever we have broken." Notice what is not said: "Actually, no one can fix it, but we who do the breaking will escape whatever the rest of you will suffer." Notice what is assumed: "Yes, the wall is there. But let us continue to drive towards the wall so that my corporation can continue to make money. The hospital will somehow put you back together again after we crash." This is a modern version of the religious con game forced on Southern slaves. We will exploit you here on earth, and God will provide you with pie in the sky. We can get on with business as usual because we possess a God of Rescue in the form of the Magician of Technology. If we possess such a god, then we do not have to change.

---

20. McKibben, "Global Warming's Terrifying New Math," para. 34.

Three Slaves and a Master (The Talents) and Fossil Fuel Executives

Tillerson's inner debate is apparently not about, "What is the right thing to do?," but more likely, "How long can we maintain our deception before reality closes in on us?" He knows that he faces a choice between changing course or leaving a legacy for which he will be massively disparaged. It remains a mystery whether this troubles him. Is he self-deceived? Does he know and not care? Does he know but chooses to deceive others, all the time well aware that the deception cannot be sustained?

Here the talentmaster of the parable looms into view. What drives *him* in his relentless pursuit of "more?" The motives of the talentmaster are no different than those of Tillerson, they are only less damaging. By garnering wealth, by taking for himself without concern for the suffering of others, he can control position, status, and at least maintain the appearance of being respected. (The curse of possessing great amounts of money is that you can never be certain whether the respect you receive is truly genuine.) We so take for granted the primacy of this ambition that we have a hard time noticing when it crosses the boundary into the criminal.

Corporate leaders share a common set of values accrued over their long history. At the heart of those values lies the belief that the accumulation of wealth is the true measure of success. They begin their careers by pledging loyalty to that pursuit, loyalty that will be tested over and again during their long climb to the top. In the eyes of fossil fuel executives, this commitment weighs the scales against humanity's well-being. To make a decision for the environment, for the integrity of the earth, entails not only forfeiting economic advantage, but also losing dignity, breaking fiduciary responsibility, betraying colleagues, sullying reputations, and losing control over their own advancement. In short, it means repudiating a lifetime of effort climbing the corporate ladder. It means joining the third slave.

Those faithful to corporate values now find themselves confronted by environmentalists who urge them to surrender both loyalty and status. Like the talentmaster, oil executives are unaccustomed to being told what to do. These men are at the top of their game. They have zero tolerance for sacrifice. Such powerful leaders buck the certainties of physics because they are unable to break out of a centuries-old ethos dictating that they focus on profits. Fossil fuel leaders are mesmerized by the widespread success of corporate governance. They have become so seduced by corporate success that they cannot overcome their propensity to provoke nature to strike back at all of us.

Jesus' Parables Speak to Power and Greed

To those of us outside profit-making imperatives, the impending collision between the use of fossil fuels and the physical limits of the earth is obvious. On the one hand is recognition of the need to limit global warming to 1.5 degrees centigrade. On the other is the "business-as-usual" perspective of fossil fuel executives, who are barreling towards that barrier like a freight train without brakes. The only way to avoid a collision is to leave trillions of dollars' worth of assets buried in the ground.

Here is the dilemma facing fossil fuel leaders: either engineer the destruction of your career or engineer the destruction of the climate. Ironically, the way out, namely, an orderly transition from carbon-intensive fuels to renewable sources of energy, would be prudent, not only in terms of climate change but also in terms of a business model that acknowledges that the continued use of fossil fuels is unsustainable. The problem is that such strategies require the loss of short-term profits, a move strongly opposed by investors.

In May 2017, at Shell Oil's annual meeting in The Hague, 94 percent of shareholders voted against the idea of setting and adhering to emissions targets advanced by a minority shareholder. One investor remarked, "No one wants Shell to put itself at a competitive disadvantage." A commentator then observed, "everyone and anyone can . . . argue that others will have a competitive advantage over them if they . . . comply. Now Exxon, etc., can argue, 'Well Shell isn't acting, so we'd better not either.' And then the entire agreement unravels."[21]

Accidents of history and chemistry have selected, from among the governing oligarchs, this particular group of executives to become the single source of disastrous consequences. While other oligarchs cause harm to many people, the oil, gas, and coal executives are positioned to undermine the entire human habitat. Thus, for example, the DuPont Corporation can knowingly pollute the bloodstreams of 99 percent of Americans with a dangerous chemical used in producing Teflon and pay out some $600 million in legal settlements, but then continue with business as usual, without incurring serious damage.[22] The worldview of both DuPont and ExxonMobil is the same. Its leaders are equally enthralled by the same ambition that puts profits before people. The only difference—and it is enormous—is in the scope of the consequences of their decisions. DuPont is constrained only by the malleable laws of legislators. Fossil fuel leaders, on the other hand,

---

21. Makortoff, "Nearly 94% of Shell Shareholders," para. 2.
22. "DuPont vs. the World," paras. 5, 76, 88.

are confronted with the unchangeable laws of physics. While executives in other industries may behave with equal disregard for human welfare, no matter how noxious their pollution, how damaging their secrecy, or how unacceptable their human costs, the consequences they face are far less dire than those faced by the fossil fuel industry. These latter control vast concentrations of carbon that for eons have been safely sequestered in the earth. Through technologies developed over several centuries, they can release that carbon into the atmosphere. This accident of history, along with carbon's propensity to create the greenhouse effect, requires them and them alone to relinquish their entire enterprise if the rest the world is to survive.

Of course, given the profound grip of the oligarchic subculture, this option is tantamount to self-destruction. It has no chance of being entertained. Rather, behind closed doors, these executives are planning to mine more than six times the amount of carbon the atmosphere can tolerate. Like the talentmaster, they refuse to give up the protected space of their corporations, the congratulations of their stockholders, and the envy of their competitors. They live in a sequestered world, oblivious to the melting of glaciers that are hemorrhaging on this earth. They deny, absolutely, their complicity in triggering a new holocaust during which not just 6 million, but millions upon millions more, will die.

Fossil fuel executives have insulated themselves from the effects of their decision-making. Allied with other oligarchs, they use their money to control major sectors of political leadership. They then use this position of power to silence minority politicians and scientists. Their success in muzzling government resistance further encourages them to intimate that, through "adaptation," they can control the reactions of nature. More likely, however, they assume they can successfully deceive consumers into believing they can achieve such control. In the process, they risk deceiving themselves.

Business history is littered with examples of incumbents who failed to anticipate a coming transition. Fossil fuel incumbents seem intent on wasting capital doing what they have always done. They would be better served to embrace change and preserve value by adopting an ex-growth strategy. Carbon Tracker Initiative Report offers these companies both a warning and a strategy for avoiding significant value destruction.[23]

---

23. Anthony Hobley, CEO of Carbon Tracker Initiative, introducing CTI's research paper, "2 Degrees of Separation."

These executives are not villains. They have become trapped by the accumulation of trillions of dollars of assets that are worthless unless mined, sold, or burned, and they are thereby a threat to all of humanity. If they are to survive as executives, they cannot afford to recognize what they are doing. As a result, they believe themselves forced into public denial, with no alternative but to wield their power to silence the voices of those who articulate the coming danger. If they are to go forward in their task of profit-making, they cannot possibly admit to the effects they are having on others.

However, while fossil fuel leaders are notable for their denial, they are not alone in putting profits over people. The essence of climate change denial centers on the conflict between wanting "more" and the limits of the earth. The widespread, shared human ambition to possess "more" unites executives in threatening humanity's well-being. That ambition is enabled by the fiction that more is always better, that self-limiting cannot possibly coexist with strategies of economic expansion.

At their base, corporate loyalties are no different than the widespread private loyalties of the middle class. We also continue to make short-term economic decisions that are to our immediate benefit, even though they contribute to our long-term destruction. Our failure to anticipate appears to be a function of distance. Were we made to feel the difficulty up close, would we jump to attention? The fact that we isolate the problem to our imaginations only leaves just enough room to put off acting.

While the perspectives of those who have never had enough obviously differ from those who have always had enough, the deprived are no more immune from the desire for the limitless "more." Hidden within the efforts to shoulder fossil fuel executives with responsibility for climate breakdown is the awareness that addressing the problem would necessitate major changes in the culture of economic expansion in which we all participate, whether in fact or in hope.

Even if we were somehow able to keep all the remaining fossil fuels buried in the ground, how quickly would renewable sources of energy be able to take their place? Could a transition occur rapidly enough to outdistance the game-changing release of "tipping points?" Too rapid a shift would clearly create serious gaps, deficiencies, and suffering. The question is: How far would we be willing to go to secure the well-being of generations to come? To what degree are we willing to endure our own discomfort? To what extent will we tolerate the inevitable unrest of others? And

Three Slaves and a Master (The Talents) and Fossil Fuel Executives

what can we do about the electoral process that responds to the immediate, not the distant?

Our difficulty grasping what is going on in Jesus' parable mirrors our difficulty in seeing what is going on around us now. Rather than face reality, we conjure a God who will rescue us. To achieve that goal, we must distort the parable. If God is not located in the behavior of the slavemaster, where in the parable is God to be found?

In his story of the talents, Jesus portrays with amazing precision the endless process, repeated down through the centuries, wherein oligarchs and their co-opted retainers accumulate wealth at the expense of others. The necessary first step in feeling what is going on is to be willing to see what is going on is. We may suppose that the position of the third slave is that of Jesus. And there, God is waiting, ever waiting, for *us* to be present in the world, so that, like third slave, *we* may find within ourselves the empathy so absent from the worldview of the slavemaster.

4

Tenants and a Landlord

The parable of the tenants and a landlord is the only one to appear in four versions. Two of these, found in the Gospel of Thomas and the Gospel of Mark, are likely independent of each other. The other two, in Matthew and Luke, are dependent on Mark. We begin with a contemporary reconstruction by John S. Kloppenborg (perhaps the major scholar of this parable). Kloppenborg's reading assumes that Jesus told this story without intending any reference to his own death. In chapter eight of his book, *The Tenants in the Vineyard*, he justifies this reconstruction.

> A man had a vineyard and leased it to tenant farmers and departed. At harvest time he sent a slave to the tenant farmers to receive from them some of the produce of the vineyard. But they seized him and beat him and sent him away empty-handed. He sent them another slave and they beat him too. Then he sent his son to them, saying, "They will respect my son." But the tenants said, "This is the heir," and they seized him and killed him.[1]

Gospel of Thomas 65

> A [. . .] person owned a vineyard and rented it to some farmers, so they could work it and he could collect its crop from them. He sent his slave so the farmers would give him the vineyard's crop.

---

[1] This reconstruction represents Kloppenborg's "general approximation of the basic structure of the original parable" (*Tenants in the Vineyard*, 272n164).

> They grabbed him, beat him, and almost killed him, and the slave returned and told his master. His master said, "Perhaps he didn't know them." He sent another slave, and the farmers beat that one as well. Then the master sent his son and said, "Perhaps they'll show my son some respect." Because the farmers knew that he was the heir to the vineyard, they grabbed him and killed him.

Beginning with Mark, the editors of the Synoptic Gospels progressively allegorized the parable to represent the rejection of the prophets and the crucifixion of Jesus. That allegory has since dominated most interpretations.

Mark 12:1–8

> A man planted a vineyard, put a fence around it, dug a pit for the wine press, and built a watchtower; then he leased it to tenants and went to another country. When the season came, he sent a slave to the tenants to collect from them his share of the produce of the vineyard. But they seized him, and beat him, and sent him away empty-handed. And again he sent another slave to them; this one they beat over the head and insulted. Then he sent another, and that one they killed. And so it was with many others; some they beat, and others they killed. He had still one other, a beloved son. Finally he sent him to them, saying, "They will respect my son." But those tenants said to one another, "This is the heir; come, let us kill him, and the inheritance will be ours." So they seized him, killed him, and threw him out of the vineyard. What then will the owner of the vineyard do? He will come and destroy the tenants and give the vineyard to others.

Jesus' story tempts listeners to assume that the landlord's request for rent is both legal and reasonable. Among the first tasks of such listeners is to step back from a too-ready agreement with that claim and ask themselves: Why would a simple levy for rent trigger a beating and murder? Could there be important reasons why the tenants would respond with such disproportionate and unexpected violence? At issue is not whether these farmers' actions are justified, but rather what from their point of view is motivating their reckless response. The answers lead us back in history: How did the landowners come to own the land they now claim? Correspondingly, how did the tenant farmers come to lose that same land?

The Galilee of Jesus' time was an agrarian economy wherein some 2 percent of the population controlled 50 percent of the wealth. Those at

Jesus' Parables Speak to Power and Greed

the top employed a two-step strategy to achieve their dominance. First, although they had lost their autonomy in subservience to Rome, they purchased the right to levy the required tribute. Second, having taxed the peasantry to the limit, they used their share of the exorbitant profits to lend money back to those same impoverished farmers. They then had only to wait for the inevitable defaults before taking ownership of the land. Time and again, peasant smallholders were forced off their ancestral lands and left with no choice but to become tenant farmers. For their part, having reduced the peasantry to subsisting on a fraction of their production, the aristocracy made off with both the property and the profit.[2] Given this history of aristocratic land-grabbing, listeners can begin to confront what is, perhaps, the central puzzle of the narrative. Why would a father who possesses abundant evidence that his distant tenant farmers violently oppose him insert his son into their midst unprotected?

The landlord is a member of an aristocratic class that has, for centuries, systematically stolen peasant land. This sequence begins with landlords wanting more, followed by their becoming obsessed with gaining even more, then breaching the bounds of justice and resorting to "legalized" land-grabbing, and finally giving credence to the same false legality they earlier used to cover up their perfidy. By so thoroughly embracing this aristocratic transformation of greed into lawfulness, the landlord has lost sight of his own participation in its ongoing violence.

The longstanding, disavowed violence of the landowning class is precisely what fuels the overt violence of the tenants. But the landlord fails to grasp the source of his tenants' rage. Instead, he mistakenly assumes that the problem is merely one of persuading his tenants to recognize the authority of his messengers; once they do so, he is certain, they will respect his claims. He is tragically mistaken. His tenants know perfectly well who he is. They have long ago judged him to be an exploiter. However, the owner refuses to allow this perception of himself to penetrate his awareness. His expectations of how his tenants will respond exclude any data at odds with his own self-perception.

It is from below, where Jesus moves, that we gain further access. The efforts to lay claim to the vineyard's produce and then to the vineyard itself may actually, in the minds of the tenants, be equivalent to repossessing what had previously been stolen from them. What's more, the violence of

---

2. For a description of the research supporting the claims of this paragraph, see Ford, *Parables of Jesus*, 31–35.

that original theft is now compounded by the insult of denying it. In the end, the tenants find themselves holding all the blame, while the landowning class, with maddening deftness, evades responsibility.

When confronted by his tenants' refusal to honor their contract, the landlord does not seek the reasons for their resistance. His only takeaway from that initial, incoherent pounding is that the status of his envoys is problematic. Because his land-holding class long ago choked off any challenges to its control, the landlord has no means of correcting his misjudgment. He has distanced himself from any knowledge of how these miscreants might actually feel about him.

Thus, he simply sends more messengers, charging them merely to reiterate his demands. They cannot avail themselves of the resources language provides. They lack authority to ask questions. They cannot reflect on the long history of aristocratic land-grabbing. They are not to explore the differing understandings about who owns what. They are not positioned to acknowledge prior injustice. They cannot sit down with the tenants and commiserate with them over their loss.

The landlord is trapped by his conviction that, having behaved lawfully, he deserves respect. He hears only himself. For their part, the tenants are not allowed to speak directly with the owner. Given no room to state their perspective and no place to maintain their dignity, their only choices are to capitulate or rebel. Language and discourse, those tools essential to unraveling misunderstanding, have been excised. To understand this tragedy, it is essential to grasp that the avenues for discourse have been systematically shut off. Thus, instead of becoming the landlord's eyes and ears, his slave messengers are merely his fists. And the landlord receives fists in return. The tenants respond to the landlord's refusal to listen by pounding out their grievances on the bloodied bodies of those unfortunate slaves. Would that the matter could rest there!

The fact that the landlord sees nothing, hears nothing, and understands nothing enrages his tenants. Though the landlord has all the data he needs to protect himself from his tenants' rage, because he has already deceived himself, he fails to act. "I am a good person who lives within the law. I will excise any awareness I might have of the lawlessness of my ancestors, or how I came to be in possession of my privilege. They do not wound me out of rage; they wound because they do not recognize me." (Ironically, they recognize him far better than he does himself.)

Jesus' Parables Speak to Power and Greed

Because he is untouched by his tenants' insults, the landlord insults *them* in what is perhaps the most profound way possible: he ignores them rather than confronting them. With enraging equanimity, he simply refuses to acknowledge how deeply his class has injured its tenants. He leaves his tenants with no alternative but to conclude that the only way to make him feel what they feel is to destroy what is valuable to him, in the same way he has destroyed what is valuable to them. His failure to comprehend them leads him to send his son unprotected into their midst. That the tenants eventually murder the landlord's son can be seen as a consequence of the landlord having earlier murdered their voice.

Can the tenants possibly believe they will get away with murder? On the face of it, nothing could be more effective in provoking the landlord's retaliation. But his failure to react to their earlier provocations has disoriented them. Even after they wounded his slaves, and thereby insulted him, the landlord did not respond with anger or with swords. Because he is convinced he is operating within the law, he fails to react to his tenants' provocation. He thereby seduces them into believing that he lacks the will to enforce his demand. His tenants mistakenly perceive him as weak.

The landlord could not anticipate that his tenants would overestimate their strength and underestimate his. He cannot imagine the level of rage fueling these dispossessed farmers, or that that rage that will propel them into ill-considered action. The landlord's need to insist that his claims are lawful combines, with lethal results, with the tenants' readiness to assume he is weak. It is difficult to characterize the violence inherent in the landlord's naiveté. When suddenly presented with the unarmed son, the tenants yield to the temptation to counter that violence with violence of their own. Only after the parable ends, when news of his son's murder eventually reaches him, will this father, in a brutal flash of illumination, confront the enormity of his error. With a corresponding naiveté, the tenants believe that they will not only escape retribution but will also reverse the long history of aristocratic land-grabbing. By failing to perceive the landlord's strength, the tenants forfeit their lives.

The violence thus disowned both by the owner and his aristocratic colleagues smolders in the tenants, until suddenly it explodes back upon the landowner. The final shared tragedy owes to unrealistic assumptions leading to ill-considered actions, cut off from any path to correct the growing misunderstandings. Reflection on that convoluted sequence can lead to an appreciation of the parable's tragic irony. The landlord's need to see himself as law-abiding enables the very destruction of the person he loves most.

The parable challenges listeners. Are you able to listen to both sides? Are you able to imagine what it would take to get them to talk to each other? How would a listener approach the landlord? Because of his power it does not occur to him to listen. How would a listener approach the tenants? They are convinced the landlord is unreachable. The tenants, like the landlord, believe in the potency of coercion to effect positive change. They say, "Let us kill the son and the vineyard will be ours." Thus, the distorted control of the landlord corrupts the response of the tenants.

With seeming equanimity Jesus outlines an impossible task. The two figures enclosed in the parable must find a way to talk with each other. The same is true with regard to climate change. Those causing climate change and those suffering from it must somehow connect, must somehow matter to each other. How can they be brought to a place where they can speak, might speak, must speak with each other? It is more difficult to reduce another person to a statistic to be manipulated when meeting face to face. What's more, empathy itself is dangerous. Given enough purchase, empathy disrupts power and shatters control. Put simply, if I empathize with you, I can no longer control you. In turn, if you understand how I feel, you undermine my ability to dismiss your feelings.

The landlord's insistence on deceiving himself forms the critical center of this story. Those listening to the parable are lured into imagining a different response, one that would require rehashing the lengthy history of how the disparities in privilege emerged. Only after acknowledging past errors does it become possible to envision future collaboration. Both face fierce resistance. The commitment to the priorities of my subgroup, at the expense of shared goals, has long been the controlling modality in the human enterprise. People do not wish to be reminded of the ways in which they achieved dominance. One way to appreciate why the landlord might distance himself from his tenants is to examine the ways we also distance ourselves from those we have dispossessed. Many countries of the third world could be understood as represented by the tenants. Instead of understanding the history of our imperialist expansion, we respond to those who protest it by blaming them. We ignore how our destruction of law has rendered them lawless.

However, if we shift to imagining what it might be like to be the tenants, and if we can get past their disproportionate response of murder, the shape of an apparently intractable conflict begins to emerge. We begin to realize how, with seeming equanimity, Jesus has entrusted to his listeners the apparently impossible task of reconciling the powerful (who have stolen) with the impoverished (who have been robbed). The two sides engaged in this narrative represent continuously warring worlds. For the landlord the war is over. "Our side won. Get used to it." For the tenants, the war continues, but they strike only if and when the landlord lets down his guard. The alienation runs so deep that both sides forget what the other is capable of. (One way listeners avoid being thrust into this quagmire is to understand this narrative to be an allegory about Jesus' crucifixion. Such an interpretation enables them to evade the work of having to imagine pathways to reconciliation. They can instead relegate responsibility for any outcome to the redemptive or vindictive intervention of God.)

A third set of tasks come to the fore. Listeners are now positioned to reconstruct a sequence leading from dispossession, to murder, and finally to the highly unpalatable prospect of the landlord giving back what he considers his lawful possession (a precise metaphor for the task confronting climate change deniers). How should one go about returning the misappropriated land to its rightful owners? Consider that the landlord will perceive this initiative as an effort to deprive him of what is his. Nonetheless, the landlord's ancestors did take that land from the tenants' ancestors. In order to acknowledge that injustice, the current landlord must be mindful of the past decisions of others, for what the victors forget the victims never forget. It also means opening ourselves up to the tenants' recrimination, which we duck by dismissing them as murderers—or, in today's parlance, as "terrorists." The immediacy of their present crimes lets us distance ourselves from our own history of crimes towards them.

The crucial element at the center of this parable is decidedly not something like other-oriented forgiveness. It is rather the landlord's insistence on self-deception. Jesus tells a story of how a competent man, following a path forged by his forebears, proceeds deeper and deeper into not knowing. Though the evidence becomes increasingly convincing, he refuses to see it. Why? Why does he not recognize the rage emblazoned on the bloodied bodies of his slaves for what it is? Because doing so would threaten his perception of himself as someone who abides by law. And that, in turn, would undermine his sense of probity when making money at the expense of others. This wealthy man would rather feel honorable than be safe. At the height of his efforts to be law-abiding, he puts into the hands of murderous strangers what is most precious to him.

In order to shift the landowner's position from disregard to respect and the tenants' from retaliation to negotiation, the listener needs to *understand* (which is different than approve) how both lawful stealing and murderous retaliation make sense to their participants. Listeners must retrace the sequence of violence that constitutes the landlord's certainty that his tenants will respect his claims. Starting with this certainty, listeners can probe behind the opening of the story to discover how the violence characteristic of the landlord's class originated in their obsession with gaining more, followed by their resort to land-grabbing, the development of a self-justifying myth of legality to cover up their perfidy and, ultimately, their astonishing but nonetheless growing belief in the truth of the very myth they have created.

One needs to imagine that the historical Jesus understood that the rage of the tenant farmers—a rage so intense that they could deny their own jeopardy and believe they would, in the end, enjoy the fruits of their hopeless rebellion—was not in response to having to pay rent, but to having, for generations, been deprived of their land. One needs to imagine that the historical Jesus was aware of the ways in which powerful people transform self-justifications into self-deceptions capable of devising false "rights." That he understood how oppressors come to believe their own lies. How believing those lies shuts off awareness of the feelings of those they dominate. And how that, in turn, leads powerful people to forfeit that which they most value.

INTERWEAVING THE PARABLE WITH MODERN DENIAL, PART I

The story begins on the bright side with the orderly process of collecting rents. Missing is the dark side of how these lands held for rent were acquired in the first place. The narrative of past events has been rewritten to serve the interests of the dominant group. But one cannot redraw the maps of feeling. The admonition to overcome injustice by "letting bygones be bygones" is futile. The fury over the past injustice has not abated; it is volatile. Like molten lava in a volcano, it lies in wait.

The story begins with the orderly processes in today's financial world, where the dominant few construct legal instruments enabling them to take control of the resources of the many. The crucial missing link in this transfer of wealth is a robust understanding of how those who dominate legalize their preying. This metamorphosis of plundering into lawfulness, made legal by phalanxes of highly paid lawyers, is what Jesus' parable so brilliantly captures. Two thousand years ago, Jesus understood that self-deception was the necessary prelude to the landowner's forfeiting what he most loves. His parable exposes what is still today most often obscure, namely, that those who deceive others must necessarily deceive themselves. And that raises the question: Have we, like the landlord, convinced ourselves that our intentions are lawful and our purposes welcome? Have we, like him, remained ignorant of how our intentions play out among those who see us as exploiters? Does Jesus' story offer resources whereby we might better understand the origins of our own miscalculations?

The dynamics of climate change require us to recognize how our very assumptions place us at a high level of danger. We imagine that our behavior is somehow lawful and that our violations are without consequence. We treat the resources we have taken as possessions. Like the landlord, we remain lethally unaware of the consequences. We fail to estimate accurately the reactions of those from whom we plunder.

Today we face climate change—an infinitely more powerful and resilient opponent. Enthralled by our narrative of endless expansion, immersed in a sense of ongoing control, and convinced of the legality of our behavior, we continue to provoke a massive retaliation. Like the landlord who sequestered himself from his tenants' anger, we do not take seriously the warnings about nature's coming retaliation. We focus on our current economic success and disallow its long-term hazards. We, too, respond by sending our children unprotected into that vortex.

Our avoidance of reality, of course, does not change that reality. The inevitable responses of the natural order to human activity remain just as dangerous. The only difference is that the violence will not come from tenants rendered murderous by being outmaneuvered; it will come from a natural order rendered retaliatory by being disregarded.

Undoing the sequence of control and profit-making deemed so essential to our own economic success is akin to undoing the sequence that led to the landlord's self-deception. Rather than facing that history, which is distasteful work, like the landlord, we shift responsibility to those who are last in line. We choose not to confront the impending but still future tragedy. But while efforts to achieve such recovery were once perceived as negotiable, in today's world, the option to negotiate no longer exists.

If we are to respond to nature's response to our overheating the earth, we will need to rethink our longstanding exploitation of fossil fuels. And that, in turn, requires us to acknowledge our earlier occupation of a large part of an otherwise empty atmospheric commons. Do we acknowledge that we have preempted the space needed by later-developing economies? Do we consider ourselves privileged because we were there earlier? Do we disavow responsibility now because the event is in the past? Our denial is born of the same desire that consumed the landlord: we want to possess more of what we have earlier determined *belongs* to us.

But we have lost sight of a critical distinction, namely, that "private property" is not an inalienable right but rather a concept invented by humans. Does the oil placed in the ground over millennia somehow "belong" to us? Is it ours to do with as we wish? Does the very fact that it is there for the taking outrank the dangers of taking it? The landlord's preoccupation with making legal his pursuit of "more" dulls him to the urgent warnings written on the bleeding bodies of his slaves. That same preoccupation renders us insensible to the even more urgent omens written on melting glaciers of distant continents.

Through wrestling with the parable's unresolved conflicts, listeners come to appreciate the same resistance experienced by those trying to negotiate the injustices of climate change. For the first time in history, we must develop a sense of shared global vulnerability. We have taken what does not belong to us. We have seized carbon that nature long ago deposited in the earth and we have released it into the atmosphere. Only by recognizing that behavior can we acknowledge our responsibility for the retaliation on deck for the entire planet. The swords of the landlord's revenge are nothing compared to the trapped rays of the sun.

No wonder we find denying reality more attractive than coping with the threat itself. Denial guards our deeply established commitment to defending the interests of our group against all the others. Denial lets us reject nature's warnings. Denial promises immediate success. Denial allows us to shift the price of inevitable failure to future generations.

Jesus' Parables Speak to Power and Greed

INTERWEAVING THE PARABLE WITH MODERN DENIAL, PART II

There is another way to view the relationship between the parable and modern events. In this reading, the disdain of blue-state voters for the experience of red-state voters parallels that of the landlord for his tenants. Like the tenants, red-state voters react by destroying those institutions that support upper-middle-class managers, while failing to notice that they also support lower-middle-class workers. This near majority of conservative, lower-middle-class, white voters is struggling to maintain itself in the face of their eroding economic status. Vulnerable to humiliation, they resist being taken advantage of. They are deeply invested in regaining respect.

Liberal voters first distance themselves from, and then write off, conservative red-state voters. The 2016 US presidential election revealed the staggering extent of this tactic. We decide that we cannot respect conservative, lower-middle-class, white voters. We scorn them for their stupidity: "How can they not see that the oligarchs, who control the politicians, have no serious interest in their welfare?"

So angered are red-state voters by our disrespect that they are driven to embrace the false respect proffered by red-state politicians. As blue-state voters have dismissed them, they in turn dismiss us—and themselves along with us. The underlying, unacknowledged sequence is as follows: (1) white workers who are dispossessed by the oligarchs are angry; (2) this anger is harnessed by politicians financed by big corporations and skillfully turned against big government; (3) blue-state disdain enhances the influence of red-state politicians; (4) by undermining government programs red-state politicians betray populist concerns for jobs and financial security. While appearing to support worker dignity, they serve oligarchic interests and are betraying the white working class.

A particularly apt analogy with the parable can be found in the combination of proximity and distance. In purple states, where the two communities live side-by-side, each refuses to have anything to do with the other. Though descended from a common heritage, they will not speak with each other. They listen to different leaders interpret the same data differently. With conviction each dismisses the other as dangerous and deluded. If you want to understand how much their group despises yours, you have only to consult how much your group despises theirs.

The parable positions liberal readers to discover their own culpability in facilitating climate denial. We are blind to the overriding impact of our disdain. When lower-middle-class conservatives reject our science, we fail to see that they are, in fact, upbraiding us for our superior attitude. Red-state rejection mirrors blue-state rejection. "You are appealing to your science while disrespecting us. In response, we will disrespect your science." The issue is not science; the issue is respect.

With the advent of climate breakdown, an unprecedented reality emerges. Because we have for the first time reached the limits of a shared earth, those who dominate and those who are dominated will suffer together. In the face of climate breakdown, those two worlds must join together, or both will be destroyed. Disdain for one another has become a modern luxury we can no longer afford.

Arlie Russell Hochschild, a sociologist from the University of California at Berkeley, is a modern Samaritan. She crossed over to the other side to investigate what it takes[3] to traverse an embedded impasse in our divided society that she called "the empathy gap." She was able to transform an entrenched position, captured in the words, "Because you will not respect me, I will not respect you" into "Because you respect me, I will respect you." Although few positions changed, many attitudes did—on both sides.

Of Hochschild's numerous insights, among the most important were the following: (1) access to understanding the "Great Paradox" was not gained by focusing on facts. It came by attending to emotions,[4] and (2) access to emotions was not gained through inquiry. It only emerged following the establishment of respect.[5]

Hochschild introduces us to Lee Davis, an eighty-two-year-old former pipe-fitter in a petrochemical plant from southwest Louisiana.[6] The story he told was not about distant fossil fuel corporations plotting to destroy the larger environment. It was rather about how he was co-opted by his immediate bosses to dump his plant's toxic waste, under cover of night, directly

---

3. Hochschild, *Strangers in Their Own Land*. Across five years she chose to leave California and reside for periods of time in Louisiana, among the reddest of red states. What she went there to try to understand was what she termed "the Great Paradox" (8). This seeming inexplicable conundrum involves why so many Louisiana residents, who have had to endure increasingly widespread, toxic pollution from surrounding oil and chemistry industries, overwhelmingly *reject* any regulation of that pollution by the federal government.

4. Hochschild, *Strangers in Their Own Land*, 15.

5. Hochschild, *Strangers in Their Own Land*, xi.

6. Hochschild, *Strangers in Their Own Land*, 25–37.

into the bayou, thus poisoning himself and his neighbors.[7] His story was not about high-level executives masking environmental treachery. It was rather about being fired for absenteeism after suffering chemical burns from an accidental release of liquid chlorine. Yet Lee Davis firmly rejects the idea of big government intervention to prevent any pollution. "[W]hile his central experience had been betrayal at the hands of industry, he now felt . . . most betrayed by the federal government."[8]

In areas polluted by the petrochemical industry, voters consistently reject any regulatory intrusions of "big government." Instead, they will absorb the unregulated consequences into their own bodies and into their own futures. Hochschild quotes one woman on the Louisiana coast who endures such pollution as saying, "Just like people have to go to the bathroom, plants do too. You can't just say, 'don't do it.'"[9]

Hochschild observes that "people on the right seemed to be strongly moved by three concerns—taxes, faith, and honor."[10] This last is probably the most important. In a transformation difficult to grasp, blue-state anxiety about global warming becomes just one more cog in the red-state experience of being disdained, while the liberals' sense of superiority becomes the engine driving conservative resentment. We simply ignore how our conceit enrages those who are less privileged. Hillary Clinton's derision of red-state voters as "a basket of deplorables"[11] was a disastrous political blunder. Although President Trump openly tells lies, he never—no matter what his actions—talks down to his supporters.[12]

Blue-state incredulity at red-state credulity deepens red-state resentment of liberal disdain. What appears to us to be a self-defeating strategy is driven far more by feelings than by fact. The proclivity in red states to ignore the findings of climate science becomes just one more piece in their effort to counter blue-state arrogance. At this turning point in the planet's future, we ridicule this choice at our peril. Our belief that we somehow deserve "superior" status is helping to destroy both them and us.

Contemporary oligarchs have skillfully mobilized red-state resentment to further their own goals. Modern blue-collar workers have long had

---

7. Hochschild, *Strangers in Their Own Land*, 29.
8. Hochschild, *Strangers in Their Own Land*, 35.
9. Hochschild, *Strangers in Their Own Land*, 166.
10. Hochschild, *Strangers in Their Own Land*, 47.
11. Reilly, "Read Hillary Clinton's 'Basket of Deplorables' Remarks," para. 1.
12. Gambino, "'I Love the Poorly Educated.'"

insufficient economic or political standing to mount an effective protest against their loss of the American dream. The oligarchs blame the workers' loss of status and consequent loss of self-worth on big government. They claim that government intrusion is responsible for frustrating workers' efforts to regain the dream. They drum into workers the idea that any government regulation, including efforts to slow climate breakdown, imposes an unacceptable limit. (Ironically, these same oligarchs rely on the provisions of big government, e.g., security, backup for large financial institutions, education of workers, infrastructure integrity, military enforcement of imperialist foreign policy, etc., to assure the accumulation of their wealth.) They equate the policies of blue states with the policies of big government. With consummate political skill, they succeed in depicting red-state discontent as ensuing from blue-state scorn. Even when the oligarchs' strategies seem transparently to trample on red-state interests, red states continue to block governmental efforts to counter oligarchic dominance. Blue states want to believe that the oligarchs' disregard for red-state interests will eventually undermine their control. However blue-state scorn is so offensive that, from a red-state perspective, quashing it takes precedence over their own self-interest.

Jesus' parable entrusts the listener to imagine how progress might be made. That is one place where the work of transforming climate denial between red and blue might begin.

5

A Slave and a Master
(The Unforgiving Slave)

The Situation

[A] **master** ... wished to settle accounts with his slaves.[1]

Scene I

(a) When he began the reckoning, one who owed him ten thousand **denarii** was brought to him; and, as he could not pay, his lord ordered him to be sold, together with his wife and children and all his possessions, and payment to be made.

(b) So the slave fell on his knees before him, saying, "Have patience with me, and I will pay you everything."

(c) And out of pity for him, the lord of that slave released him and forgave him the debt.

---

1. See above p. 23n1.

A Slave and a Master

Scene II

(a) But that same slave, as he went out, came upon one of his fellow slaves who owed him one hundred denarii; and seizing him by the throat, he said, "Pay what you owe."

(b) Then his fellow slave fell down and pleaded with him, "Have patience with me, and I will pay you."

(c) But he refused; then he went and threw him into prison until he would pay the debt.

Scene III

(a) When his fellow slaves saw what had happened, they were greatly distressed, and they went and reported to their lord all that had taken place.

(b) Then his lord summoned him and said to him, "You wicked slave! I forgave you all that debt because you pleaded with me. Should you not have had mercy on your fellow slave, as I had mercy on you?"

(c) And in anger his lord handed him over to be tortured until he would pay his entire debt.

(Matt 18:23–34 NRSV)
(Author's changes in boldface.)

A BEGINNING CAVEAT

Before entering the parable, one must question the impossibly huge loan of 10,000 talents. If the amount stands as written, the narrative becomes fantastic. Herod Antipas, who was able to impose on Galilee and Perea an annual tribute of about 200 talents, would have been fifty years repaying.[2] Such hyperbole clearly supports Matthew's allegorical interpretation: he understands the parable to be describing both how a gracious God forgives and how Christians in response ought also to forgive. But

---

2. Josephus, *Ant.* 17:318–320.

scholar Martinus C. de Boer proposes that, in order to enhance his allegorical reading, Matthew altered a single word to vastly inflate the amount owed. He changed the original "denarii" to "talents," and then he promoted the slavemaster to king.[3] I agree with de Boer and, using boldface, have edited the text accordingly.

THE SLAVE

A primary means for probing the attitudes of a superior is to empathize with the experience of an inferior. The underling knows better than anyone who his superior actually is. In this story, the behavior of a slave toward his weaker colleague echoes his master's control. All that is lacking for him to express that control is sufficient power. Were he to gain access to his overlord's power, he would almost certainly replicate his master's dominance. He would respond by setting aside disappointment, moving through rage, and then settling into being coercive. It is not easy to understand why someone would become coercive after being coerced; nonetheless the phenomenon is widespread.

In the agrarian economy of Jesus' time, the only way to make large profits was to lend money to marginal peasants, and then, when they defaulted, to confiscate their land.[4] One likely reason the slave lost control over his loan was that he was insufficiently ruthless in targeting vulnerable outliers and taking their land.

The value of 10,000 denarii in today's terms is estimated at about $1,200,000.[5] It would take the slave considerable time to lose that much money and considerable effort to mask that failure. (It would also take considerable obtuseness on the slavemaster's part for him to remain ignorant of his trusted subordinate's inability to function.) The longer the slave's distressing disfunction went unchallenged, the larger the debt grew. And the

---

3. De Boer, "Ten Thousand Talents?," 214–32.

4. For a detailed description of the aggrandizing strategies of the agrarian aristocracy of Jesus' time, see Ford, *Parables of Jesus*, 31–35.

5. As illustrated in the parable of the vineyard workers, one denarius was the customary minimum wage for a day's labor. Excluding the sabbath (52 out of 365 days), leading to 313 workdays, one day laborer would have to work 31.9 years to make 10,000 denarii (10,000 denarii divided by 313 workdays a year). Calculating $15/hour minimum wage or $120 day in contemporary wages, today's day laborer would make $37,800 a year (315 times $120). 31.9 years times $37,800/yr. comes to $1,206,000, which is as reasonable an estimate as any for the modern value of 10,000 denarii.

more the debt grew, the harder the slave would have had to work to cover up his delinquency. The consequent build-up of anxiety, suddenly released, would likely have much to do with the slave's egregious miscalculation in dealing with his colleague.

In losing the large amount of money entrusted to him, the slave resembles other parable subordinates—the younger son who wasted his father's inheritance, the manager who squandered his employer's property, and the slave who refused to invest his master's money. In each one of these cases the failure of the subordinate to function as he should can be traced directly to deficits in the superior's way of being. The same is true for this parable.

One way to engage this narrative is to notice the slave's dangerous disregard for his own well-being. The listener then has the option to move from being impressed by the slave's failure to imitate his master's generosity (the place where most understandings of this story begin) to pondering the slave's apparent stupidity. Although well-placed and skillful enough to win a large loan from his master, this competent man makes an awesome mistake. Having just been released from debt and destitution, in easy view of his recently magnanimous lord he cashiers his fellow slave.

The slave's thoughtless behavior makes sense only if some other reality takes precedence over the one immediately apparent. His seeming stupidity may in fact represent loyalty to a prior set of values. Throughout their lives both men have served the order of a society of slaves and masters. Until now neither has relaxed the control essential to its maintenance. Whether or not the slave can manage it, he knows perfectly well that he is supposed to block out empathy in order to crush the weaker partner. Such ruthlessness was commonplace up and down the social spectrum; no one would have thought to raise a finger in protest.

At the moment he no longer confronts debt, the slave is faced with an impossible quandary. He has somehow to integrate the generosity shown him with the longstanding expectation of ruthlessness. He is utterly unprepared for his lord's shocking magnanimity; he simply cannot comprehend it. He may, in fact, feel overwhelmed. The ability to imagine how another person might feel is born of having others imagine how you feel. The slave has never known that experience. Thus, for him the rush of released anger easily takes precedence over any exercise in empathy. Not only is he unable to connect what has just been done for him with what he should now be doing, he fails to anticipate how his refusal to emulate his master will provoke the latter's retaliation. As this sudden, unexpected riptide starts to pull him under, he tries to hang on to the only reliable way of relating he has ever known: he grabs for his colleague's throat.

His attack on his hapless colleague may be seen as his best effort at squaring the circle. If the world is no longer made up of "users" and "used," of what could it possibly be made? Rather than opting for this totally new way of being, he elects to mimic the earlier ways of his master. If this slavemaster will no longer maintain the established order—an order which until this moment has been utterly predictable—then the slave himself, ignoring his personal safety, will wrench that order back into place.

The slave is now doing to his fellow precisely what his master has previously done to him. He becomes the one who chokes as he himself was choked; he turns into the very person he so intensely hates. He acts to force back into place those long-standing patterns of control that have been the bedrock of his reality. When he chokes, demands, and imprisons, the slave is in fact imitating his master—not, however, the incomprehensible, "new" master, but rather the merciless lord he has always known (and who will soon reappear).

THE SLAVEMASTER

The slavemaster has always dominated his slave. Yet he has somehow remained ignorant of his slave's increasing loss of control. Thus, he is blind to his slave's mounting anxiety. It staggers the imagination how he could be so clueless about that in which he has so much invested. Even more importantly, the master does not sense his slave's rage when he cannot or will not function the way his master wants. When suddenly released from debt, abruptly freed of crippling anxiety, and unable to attack his master, the slave attacks his fellow. The master is not only oblivious to the fact that the attack was meant for him, but he also fails to realize that he provoked it in the first place. How? Most immediately by ignoring the slave, but most effectively by a lifetime of exploiting weaker others, including the slave himself.

The master's self-deception is astonishing. He assumes he can control his slave's inner life. In parallel fashion, he believes he can communicate release across the enormous barrier of dominance he has himself erected. He becomes enraged that his slave does not imitate him. Not for one moment does this lord suppose that, when grabbing and choking his fellow, his subordinate is, in fact, imitating him. In being so astonishingly mean-spirited, the slave is simply doing what his master, until this very moment, has always done. The slave has not yet been able to assimilate this new, strange, and unexpectedly generous lord; his imagination remains governed by a lifetime of experience with his old, familiar, and chronically domineering master, the one who never once loosened his grip—and the one who is about to tighten it once again.

> his lord ordered him to be sold, together with his wife and children ... out of pity for him, the lord of that slave released him and forgave him the debt. ... in anger his lord handed him over to be tortured ...

The rapidity of the slavemaster's mood swings is breathtaking. Within a brief span of time, he moves from the cruelty of breaking up a family (brooking no delay), to compassionate release (extending extraordinary largess), to vengeful torturing (allowing no escape). How can such different attitudes arise in such rapid succession from within the same person? One answer, in brief, is that the master tried to take a short-cut to achieve change—and got slammed.

By forgiving the debt the master makes an extraordinary gesture. But he also appears seduced by the supposed potency of his initiative. His anger at the failure of his generous act suggests that he was convinced it would be effective. It may be that an inaccurate expectation borne of dominance accounts for his shifting moods. He does indeed seem to hope, with surprising naiveté, that with a single, masterful stroke he should be able to dent and even flatten those misshapen attitudes long hardened into the very foundation of a society of masters and slaves.

The master's act of releasing is so caught up in his ongoing assumption of dominance that its effectiveness is vitiated. The slave resists his master's new attempt to coerce him by imitating his master's habitual domination. By focusing on the slave's ungrateful response, the story draws attention away from the master. Thus, listeners fail to perceive that the master's inability to let go of his own life of coercion renders him impotent to release his slave from the same.

Up until that moment, the master's life had been dedicated to coercion. We are left not knowing why he chose to make an exception, why he tried to enter this unknown territory. The parable focuses not on antecedents but rather on consistency. The slave gets universal blame for not being able to negotiate such a high-speed U-turn. Often unacknowledged is how much trouble the master himself experiences when engaged in the same sudden maneuver.

This lord's manner of acting is certainly appropriate to the behavior of slavemasters, but it is ill-fitted to the work of releasing. By remaining the sole arbiter of the new order as well as the old, he excludes any experience other than his own. By dictating rather than participating, he permits only compliance. By his generosity, he distances himself further from the realities of his own dominance. He attempts to release his slave's debt without acknowledging his own, namely, his obligation to recognize the contradiction between his newly minted behavior and his chronically insistent control. The master—and many listeners with him—simply assigns this backbreaking work to his slave. His slave should do all the changing; he should have to do none.

From within his new role as the one who releases, the master looks to transform, in a single moment, the harshness of a slave culture centuries in the making. The parable outlines a sequence. All his life the master has choked the slave. Then he suddenly releases the slave. Then the slave goes out and chokes his fellow. What is going on? Within the new paradigm, the master retains the old—he remains master. When releasing, he stays in charge. He does not wonder or ask, he declares. Precisely because he acts as master, that is, unilaterally, he fails to adopt what may be the only way available to enable another to change, namely, to be aware of and affirm the other's experience. The top-down nature of his initiative ignores his slave's need gradually to come to terms with a strange, dangerous, new way of being. By hoping to engender a releasing attitude while, at the same time, remaining in control, the master undermines his own potency. Indeed, the master's condemning words, "Should you not have had mercy . . . as I had mercy on you?" appear very close to the words he has just condemned, namely, "Pay what you owe!"

The master's judgment is warped by his power. He comes to believe in coercion's effectiveness. In so doing, he foregoes the ability to empathize. At the same time, he misunderstands his slave, he deceives himself. And thus, he finds himself in the crosshairs of the same ineffectiveness and consequent rage he has instilled in his underling.

Although one does not have to suppose that the master released the debt in order to render his slave a more generous person, both the master and many listeners agree that such a transformation ought to have occurred. Here the listeners, along with the master and Matthew, are caught in a trap.

They find themselves supporting the very act the master has condemned, namely, punishing someone for a failed obligation. This time, however, the debt owed is not 100 denarii. It is, rather, the obligation that the slave, ready or not, should imitate his master's unexpected generosity. Together with the slavemaster, these listeners say to the slave, "I will ignore your capacities in favor of my own expectations. I will imprison you until you repay an obligation that I have, without warning or preparation, decided to enforce. I will do to you exactly what I am punishing you for having done."

The slave does to his fellow what the master has always done to him. Masters have always dominated slaves; this beast has careened down through the centuries unopposed. So, who is responsible to halt it? The little guy at the end of the line? Does it in fact fall to him to do the prodigious work that everyone before him has failed even to imagine, much less confront? The irony here is profound. This master—and many listeners with him—is saying to this slave, "You should be able to overturn in a moment what I have been unable to face in a lifetime," namely, the deep-seated attitudes of coercion that result when one person remains in complete control of another. When the master releases his slave's debt, listeners are drawn into having to make a truly remarkable choice. For at this moment, they must decide whether this lord's singular act of generosity indeed has the power to wrest apart ancient slavery's iron law of ruthlessness.

Approached in these terms, the problems the parable offers are formidable. How indeed does one reconcile the open-ended process of release with the human propensity to dominate? How is it possible to bridge the gulf between the world of control, with its fixed requirement of compliance, and the world of releasing, which necessarily requires first experiencing and then acknowledging how the other person feels? How can the master possibly recognize the deep-seated effects on both himself and his slave of his own total buy-in to the corrupted society of masters and slaves? How far, then, might the master's affronted rage have strayed from its true source?

INTERWEAVING THE PARABLE WITH MODERN DENIAL

A major theme in this parable is how the slave does to his weaker colleague what his master has done to him. That urge, built up over a lifetime, is so potent it trumps any desire to imitate the master's newfound generosity. Likewise, today, because they are unable to challenge the oligarchs, persons deprived by the greed of the oligarchs will instead attack those less fortunate than themselves. This parable becomes a brilliant commentary on those white lower-middle class workers who give their allegiance to powerful oligarchs who, in turn, secretly abuse them while openly vilifying available scapegoats. Like the slave, these underclass workers learn to choke their more vulnerable colleagues—blacks, Hispanics, immigrants, those on welfare. Their need to hurt *someone* becomes an obsession. They are like the playground bully who, unable to fight his punitive father, searches out a weaker schoolmate.

The oligarchs, for their part, are pleased to support this scapegoating. Their message to these American workers, whose income has been flat or declining, consistently encourages workers to vent their anger. "Big government puts all these people ahead of you in the line for the American dream." Big government, which is bad for the oligarchs in terms of regulation, instead becomes bad for workers in terms of discrimination. The super elite meld these separate perspectives into one. The strategy is brilliant and successful. The oligarchs redirect rage going upwards towards themselves into rage going downward towards immigrants and people of color. This fool's gold of seeming caring sits side by side with the satisfaction of retribution.

The oligarchs take one further step. They also focus worker discontent on the middle management class, often made up of Democrats. "Those middle-class managers are finally getting what they deserve. Let their jobs and prospects be wrecked the same way as ours have been." We so much want those blue-state snobs to get theirs that we cannot recognize that the same powerful people who will harm them will also do us harm.

Donald Trump's personal discontent mirrors the discontent of his white, lower-middle class supporters. His own history renders him unusually adept at connecting with them emotionally. And he commands the power to retaliate in ways they wish they could. On a nationwide scale, Trump broadcasts what each supporter privately feels. Altogether obscured is how his discontent has nothing to do with theirs, and how his attitudes and actions have nothing to do with ameliorating their pain. In a bizarre accident of history, he is able to translate his utterly self-centered ambition into the semblance of caring about the legitimate needs of great numbers of people.

The master's forgiveness of his slave's debt does not in any way change his fundamental orientation towards greed. Whatever his motivations, he has in no way released his stranglehold on the surrounding peasantry. Big

Oil may make feints at conservation, like that made by British Petroleum when it ran a green campaign for a time at the beginning of this century, but they are cosmetic. We are bereft of any power in the temple of greed able to overcome the essential premise that one should take as much as one can. Lost is the irony that altruism is today's greatest form of self-interest.

The parable positions listeners to feel the ways the slave, who himself has known a lifetime of domination, fails to grasp how his weaker colleague might feel when dominated. How can the slave not relate to someone who is undergoing the same experience as himself? The modern parallel is how today's workers cannot see that, in discriminating against people of color, they are mirroring the oligarchs' discrimination against themselves. If they could empathize, they would see. But the satisfactions of class solidarity and retaliation defeat any tendencies towards empathy.

Nor are the managerial elites of the blue states home free. Right now, we are frightened and angry at the willingness of the red-state, white, working class to support the destruction of our democratic institutions. What we have not realized, and what the parable so deftly encourages us to see, are the ways in which their destructive reaction to us is in direct response to how they perceive themselves as having been deprived by us. When the slave chokes his colleague, he is signaling to the world what his master has done to him. He is saying that his master's release of his debt has not released him from a lifetime of abuse. In a similar vein, we believe we can use the facts of science to effect change in red-state voters without having to deal with their perception of how our economic success has deprived them of theirs. When voters in red states take satisfaction in the destruction of our shared institutions, we do not recognize the extent to which we are being upbraided for our sense that we deserve our success, while they deserve their failure.

A huge amount is at stake in this wholesale scattering of anger and angst. By aggrandizing worker wealth and redirecting worker rage downwards towards immigrants and people of color, and outward towards the middle class, the oligarchs dissipate anxiety about the deadly approach of climate change. While they keep us busy despising each other, climate breakdown is coming to choke us all.

If we release our grip on the prevailing interpretation of this parable, we may discover ourselves drawn to consider further the difficulties of entering the kingdom of God, that is, of participating in God's desire for the world. We may discover that we are being invited to experience more closely and plumb more deeply the complex dimensions of Jesus' aphorism, "How hard it will be for those who have wealth (that is, for those whose lives are controlled by the ability to control others) to enter the kingdom of God" (Mark 10:23)

6

A Manager and a Rich Man
(The Dishonest Steward)

The Situation

There was a rich man who had a manager,

Scene I

and charges were brought to him that this man was squandering his property. So he summoned him and said to him, "What is this that I hear about you? Give me an accounting of your management, because you cannot be my manager any longer."

Scene II

Then the manager said to himself, "What will I do, now that my master is taking the position away from me? I am not strong enough to dig, and I am ashamed to beg. I have decided what to do so that, when I am dismissed as manager, people may welcome me into their homes." So, summoning his master's debtors one by one, he asked the first, "How much do you owe my master?" He answered, "A hundred jugs of olive oil." He said to him, "Take your bill, sit down quickly, and make it fifty." Then he asked another, "And how much do you owe?" He replied, "A hundred containers of wheat." He said to him, "Take your bill and make it eighty."

Scene III

And his master commended the dishonest manager because he had acted shrewdly.

(Luke 16:1b–8a NRSV)

The story of a manager and a rich man (the dishonest steward, Luke 16:1b–8a) tells of an estate manager who is publicly praised but privately disparaged, while his rich employer emerges unscathed. It traces the irreversible, downward trajectory of a mutually dependent but unequal relationship. It is a subtle story. It does not explain the manager's collapse. His subsequent efforts to survive appear to both the rich man and listeners alike as a betrayal.

At the same time, however, this narrative can be seen as describing how a powerful person—steeped in a culture of domination characterized by the loss of empathy—undermines shared loyalties, provokes a loss of control, pushes aside, and then discards a subordinate. The parable assigns listeners the work of breaking free from this normative world of power. It invites them to reflect on both their own participation in that world and their temptation to disparage resistance to it. For those who protest the denial of climate change, the story's potential for a massive double take can serve as a valuable resource: it portrays some of the ways in which the powerful effectively marginalize that protest.

In this story a wealthy man gives his estate manager the authority to act on his behalf in negotiating contracts with outside borrowers. Across the social distance separating them, these two protagonists function as interdependent collaborators. The rich man trusts his manager to invest considerable amounts of money. The manager, in turn, relies completely on the rich man for his well-being and security. This level of mutual dependency and trust is the most intense between a superior and subordinate found in any of Jesus' nine extant narrative parables, with the exception of the prodigal son.

The parable begins by confronting listeners with an unexplained, perplexing problem: this formerly prudent estate manager, whose security is wholly dependent on his employer's goodwill, has for some time been wasting his master's property. This confounds listeners. This manager is neither criminal nor malevolent. Why would a man who later exhibits an intense concern for his own security have been so careless about that same security?

Moreover, this man is squandering his master's goods. He is not stealing them. Stealing requires calculation. "Squandering" implies an out-of-control disregard for his own welfare. (The same Greek verb, *hipopiadzo*, is used in Luke 15:13 to describe the prodigal son's wasting of his inheritance.) As Jesus' original listeners knew well, the life span of a day laborer was far shorter than that of an estate manager. Thus, the manager has for some time been endangering not only his position but his life. As listeners, do we acknowledge these difficulties? Or do we conclude that they are irrelevant, that the story has only a single point? If so, what is the point? The answer to that question continues to elude interpreters who strain to imagine what it might be.

If, instead, we were to pay careful attention to that which seems to make no sense, we would be obliged to account, somehow, for what caused the manager to move from careful management to a loss of control. At the end of the story his employer will praise him for his skill at self-preservation, describing him as someone able to act sensibly, thoughtfully, prudently, wisely, shrewdly (Luke 16:8, in the Greek, *phronimos*). But it is too late. By then he has destroyed both his career and probably his life.

Parables challenge us to create consistency out of hints and fragments. Without fully realizing it, we tend to fill in their artfully crafted gaps with our own assumptions. Or, without noticing it, we sidestep any incoherence. In identifying the contours of our own experience, it helps to become aware of where we are focusing our attention. The same is true with this parable. The crucial initial decision in addressing the parable is the degree to which we choose to focus attention on that which makes no sense. That gap, or enigma, is a portal to a story hidden in plain view. However, in order to find the nuances, listeners must resist the temptation to turn the rich man into a

Jesus' Parables Speak to Power and Greed

God figure. Once that happens, like the rich man himself, hearers will miss the part he may have played in the manager's breakdown.

The parallel between the rich man's disregard of the evidence of his subordinate's collapse and the listener's disregard of the voids in the rich man's behavior is truly remarkable. Just as the overlord has stopped listening to his underling, listeners have stopped listening to the overlord. If they are to perceive some relationship between the manager's squandering of his lord's property and the lord's squandering his concern for his manager, listeners must overcome their inclination to ignore the rich man's neglect.

Each man appears invested in the other only to the extent that the other serves his purpose. However, while the rich man can survive without his manager, the reverse is not true. This is where the imbalance of power plays a critical role. Since the manager has only his lord to protect him, he is highly attuned to any fluctuations in his superior's approval; his self-confidence depends entirely on his employer's regard. Although neither man appears burdened by guilt at the prospect of hurting the other, their power relationship determines that the rich man's loyalty to his subordinate becomes the condition for the latter's loyalty to him. But for some reason, what for the manager has all along been essential, for the rich man has now become negligible. He is no longer interested in his subordinate.

How can the rich man not realize that his manager is wasting his goods? This oversight occurs at the very heart of that which engages his attention: making money. It's rather as though his precious yacht has sprung a leak, and he keeps sailing on, oblivious. (Our not knowing similarly occurs at the very center of what should engage our attention: maintaining a livable world. We do not perceive that the oligarchs are wasting our world. By its gradual collapse, our world is trying to tell us.)

The rich man wants a solution (the firing) without understanding the problem (his neglect).

Three times Jesus supplies evidence of this man's neglect:

1. The rich man is unaware that his manager is throwing his property to the winds; others have to tell him. How could he have remained so completely ignorant of such obvious behavior? His subordinate is not skillfully deceiving him. He is desperately out of control. What happened to the earlier, thoughtful interactions between the two men?

2. When calling his manager to account, the rich man displays no curiosity about why his subordinate has so thoroughly undermined

the trust that had grown up between them. His empathy is weak; his self-interest is weaker. Given their prior relationship, one would think the man of wealth would want to find out why his subordinate broke that trust. His failure to be curious is itself curious. He has invested resources, effort, trust, and authority in his subordinate. By his indifference, he is throwing these investments to the winds.

Here is a critical moment in the story. Because the man of wealth so thoroughly pushes his manager away, he cuts off any chance he might have had to discover his own role in what happened. He never allows his manager to tell him, "Somehow you seemed to stop valuing my services. I felt you were neglecting me, so I just gave up. My wasting your goods was in fact my desperate effort to get you to see me, to come back, to stabilize me." (Here the manager is very like a delinquent adolescent who has been ignored by his parents.)

3. As if to underline the degree of his prior neglect, the rich man reveals no concern for how his formerly trusted manager might feel upon being dismissed. He has no awareness of how he might be provoking his employee's rising distress. Thus, after firing him, he foolishly leaves intact his subordinate's authority to summon and negotiate with his substantial debtors.

The rich man's neglect flourishes unrestrained by concern for his manager's well-being. In this employer's eyes, his employee should be able to function without receiving emotional support or recognition. The manager's response to this vacuum in his emotional world is confusing to himself, his master, and the listeners. The rich man ignores his own loss of interest and instead assumes his subordinate is intentionally incompetent. Like oligarchs who accept no responsibility for the earth's collapse, he convinces himself that he has nothing to do with the collapse of his subordinate.

Neither man perceives the true source of the trouble. That work is left to parable-listeners. But listeners, too, uncritically accept the controlling narrative of the elites. They tend to identify with the rich man. They pass over evidence of his increasing emotional distance from his dependent manager.

Listeners are called upon to enter "from below," that is, to notice the particular ways the manager might be responding to the rich man's neglect. The manager despairs when he senses that he is losing the strong man's attention and regard. At this point, is he likely to risk an open demand? It is not safer to flail in an effort to attract the rich man's fading awareness? One would think the latter might notice the impact on his investments. But, strikingly, none of his subordinate's efforts has the least effect. The rich man remains oblivious to the collapse of his trusted underling.

Though both men flounder, only the manager is held responsible. Only he faces destitution. We are at a critical moment in the story. Following his failed efforts to recapture his master's regard, the manager now stands bereft of resources. Neither competence nor collapse has proven effective. Only after others prod the rich man, only after his lord finally calls him to account, does the manager find the resources to reshape his own helplessness. Following his master's curt, self-absorbed rejection, the manager at last comprehends that neither competence nor collapse will reawaken his master's lost regard. He finally grasps the horrific fact that the well is dry. He now understands that further digging is useless. He jumps to attention. He reverts to his previous shrewdness. He must look elsewhere for water.

To whom can he possibly turn? In his terror at having lost his security, the manager now crosses the boundary into treachery. At this moment all is lost. He regresses from trying to win trust through competence to trying to buy trust through bribery. He gives up on his own earlier but now-useless strategy of being reliably competent, and instead adopts the rich man's strategy of using wealth to control compliance. Ironically, his despairing mimicry of his master forever brands him as "dishonest." His crisis response will be seen, correctly, as betrayal by those with whom he seeks to curry favor. In his quest for employment, he has rendered himself unemployable. No one will ever again trust him with the management of their money. The sequence beginning with the rich man's withdrawal ends with his manager's self-destruction.

In one final act of neglect, the rich man enables that self-destruction. He becomes as inattentive to his own interests as he has been to those of his manager. He fails to inform his wealthy debtors in a timely manner that he has dismissed his subordinate. Had they been informed about the latter's being stripped of authority, no one among the debtors would have dared to alter his bill. But the manager's summons to these debtors outpaces any alert from his lord. The rich man thereby enables his manager to walk into a trap. The latter imagines he is assuring his future security. But while his debtors will for a time provide him with favors, no one will be taken in by him.

This reality of the manager's coming destruction is nowhere evident in the rich man's final praise. His lord portrays him as acting shrewdly when he is doing exactly the opposite. Once it becomes public knowledge that he left his dismissed manager with enough authority to defraud him, the rich man has two options. He can openly acknowledge his shameful stupidity. Or he can champion his manager's rediscovered astuteness. As a prince among ancient spin doctors, he chooses the latter. Here we are introduced to the skill with which some among the wealthy can use their power to escape responsibility. He steps out of the shadows of his neglect to praise his employee's self-defeating behavior. With impressive skill, he uses false praise to avoid acknowledging his prior neglect. He even seems to embrace his own deception.

In the end the manager is destroyed, while the rich man departs, confidently blaming and publicly praising his victim. Although aggrieved, he appears to exit the parable convinced of his rectitude. He has reduced his manager to incompetence—all the while declaring the unfortunate subordinate to be the one responsible. In the shambles, the rich man's prestige in the community is tarnished, the debtors' relationship with their patron is compromised, and the manager's position and eventually his life is sacrificed.

Listeners must labor at length to find coherence in a tragedy so skillfully disguised. They are called upon to probe the inner workings of the parable with a sustained attention notably absent in the characters themselves. The skill of the narrator is extraordinary.

INTERWEAVING THE PARABLE WITH MODERN DENIAL

The question of neglect is *the* central question of this parable. How does the rich man come to ignore his vitally important manager? Both the neglect itself and the reasons for it remain shrouded. In their place is the flailing, reprehensible response of the manager. In a relationship of unequal power, the manager is silenced, blamed, and allowed to fail. His protest is seen as incompetence. At the same time, the rich man's incompetence remains unacknowledged. As is regularly the case with the longer narrative parables, the dominance of an overlord distorts the voice of an underling. Listeners readily blame the underling and vindicate the overlord. What is needed—namely, affirmation of interest and concern from the overlord—is lacking.

Jesus' Parables Speak to Power and Greed

The rich man has distanced himself from a relationship situated at the very heart of his enterprise. He has a subordinate on whom he relies and who, in turn, relies on him. Yet he has somehow failed to recognize that his trusted subordinate is floundering. Others have to tell him: "What is this I hear about you?" How do others see what he does not? How can he possibly not realize that his manager has been busily flinging his wealth to the winds? The parable does not say. All we know is that the rich man is preoccupied with something other than his collaboration with his manager. For some reason he has stopped engaging. He has stopped interacting. Even more importantly, the rich man appears unaware of the impact of his lack of awareness. The rich man has the right to his neglect, but he does not have the right to deny its consequences.

Like the rich man, we are neglecting the future victims of our decisions. The victims-to-be of climate change have almost no purchase on our imagination. We readily rebuff their aborning protest. When we encounter the challenge of fifteen-year-olds, we need to hear them speaking for the generations that will be beginning to feel the impact of climate change. How can we so easily ignore the vast array of human beings yet to be born who will be totally dependent for the quality of their lives upon decisions we make now?

As with the manager, their lack of power impedes their ability to make themselves heard. And, just as we are unable to see the rich man's neglect as the source of the manager's incompetence, so we are unable to see how our neglect of these future citizens will inevitably result in their dysfunction. Our lack of empathy is in direct proportion to our power.

We have some awareness that our possessions will result in the dispossession of others. That issue is clearly demonstrated by the disappearance of available space in the atmospheric commons. By taking more space for ourselves, we leave less for the dispossessed. What we are doing now mirrors what we will do in the future. Rich nations have already positioned themselves to deprive poor nations. They are pressuring poor nations to shoulder the costs of adaptation for deficits they did not create. The parallel to the parable is found in the rich man's utter disregard for the impact of his neglect on his dependent subordinate.

Climate change will exacerbate divisions already developing between the haves and have-nots. Growing scarcities of water and food, the spread of disease, and the creation of a vast array of climate immigrants will put enormous pressure on existing institutions. It will fragment people across the globe into competing, warring groups.

The parable prompts listeners to wonder why they afford the rich man the authority to dismiss a manager whose loyalty has been skewed by his neglect. The rich man seemingly has every justification for his action. Yet his lack of curiosity when dismissing his manager hints at his need to remain ignorant of his own role. Are listeners lured into overlooking their complicity in the rich man's illusion of innocence? And their current complicity in excluding future victims?

The gateway into this conundrum is to assume that the manager's life-threatening neglect of his duties is a consequence of something more than carelessness—something substantial enough to disrupt even the most basic instinct for self-preservation. In effect the manager is saying, "I cannot function without some evidence of your interest in my well-being." This theme is widespread within families and across societies. Whatever the reasons for the rich man's neglect, his loss of interest in his dependent manager sucks oxygen out of the room. And it has consequences that cannot immediately be discerned. Parable-listeners are invited to step in and take note of the deadly grasping by someone in power—and then to face the difficult decision about where to situate themselves in relation to future inhabitants of this planet.

This parable depicts the infiltration of withdrawal. The manager does not know what has hit him: his well-being is being undermined by absence. A mentor who had been so much a part of his life has stopped responding. What had been present has been subtly distanced. The lord's inexplicable withdrawal of interest renders the manager incompetent. Because the rich man supplies no explanation for his disappearance, the manager must come up with his own. He concludes that *he* must somehow be responsible, that he must fix what he has not broken. This assumption becomes his downfall.

The manager's inability to cope with this precarious position (which in the end, ironically, is praised by his master), is the consequence of the rich man's refusal to recognize the effects of his own withdrawal. The manager is forced to act dangerously because the rich man has withdrawn his previously reliable support. That the manager should destroy his chances for survival is the price imposed on him by the rich man in order to escape his own responsibility. In effect, the rich man has changed the terms of their engagement. "You, manager, should be able to function as well as you always have but without my presence and interest." The manager responds,

"Since I cannot rely on your interest, I will *make* others interested in me." He turns to something he can control, in this case bribery. As those he bribes do not like being controlled, he will eventually be completely ruined.

Voiceless people present today foreshadow the position of vast numbers in a future filled with deprivation. As we ignore them today, so they will forget us tomorrow. Instead, they will focus their energy on depriving members of nearby warring subgroups. We, the original authors of their deprivation, will have been long forgotten.

What is striking in this parable is how completely the rich man controls his manager's sense of well-being. The manager is isolated from his peers. He has had no choice but to place his self-esteem into the rich man's hands, thus leaving himself vulnerable to his overlord's loss of interest. That neglect, like the abdication of the prodigal father, leads the manager to squander his master's resources. The manager's only means of expressing the devastating loss of the rich man's presence, which has heretofore anchored his sense of competence, is to cease functioning.

One would think that the rich man, although lacking concern for his manager's well-being, might at least have attended to his own economic interests. The distracted manager was not emotionally capable of skilled deception. His profligate behavior was readily discernible (as is today's out-of-control wasting of the earth's resources). Had he been aware of his subordinate's loss of control, the rich man could have intervened in a timely fashion. But the man is stunningly obtuse. By failing to see what is right in front of him, he renders himself incapable of intervening. Like a passive victim, he stands immobilized on the sidelines. The parable does not challenge or criticize his choice. It simply documents the fact. Listeners are left to move forward into the inevitable tragedy by themselves. In so doing, they must wrestle with the question which neither superior nor subordinate can address, namely, *"How could the rich man not see what was going on?"*

The rich man's priority—profit-making—should at least have alerted him to the fact that his manager was wasting those profits. But for some reason, he is incapable of looking after his own interests. That he lifted his hand off the tiller appears to imply some needful distraction rather than careless inattention. While the manager is contorted with anxiety, the rich man appears preoccupied with shutting down.

In the contemporary world, modern followers also suffer a loss of place. Like the manager, they lack the ability to generate self-esteem. They rely on their leaders to overcome their inability to stand on their own and cannot function when that leadership fails them. For their part, by declaring the actual attacking monster a "hoax," leaders render themselves useless. Still, they say what their followers most want to hear. And once those followers are no longer capable of determining what is true, and thus depend upon their leaders for access to reality, a leader's move into denial leaves those followers rudderless. They do not protest because they cannot bear the thought of losing their leader. Their praise is the price of his presence. They have become oblivious to the extreme danger of buying into his perspective.

The loss of his employer's attention leaves the manager floundering. The disregard of climate change-deniers likewise leaves future generations floundering. Those consumed by the need to deceive themselves have no capacity left to consider the fate of future generations. Future generations, for their part, have no path to elicit concern for their well-being from those present today—a concern which has to be activated now if it is to be effective.

7

The Poor and a Householder
(The Great Banquet)

The Situation

Someone gave a great dinner and invited many.

Scene I

At the time for the dinner he sent his slave to say to those who had been invited
 "Come, for everything is ready now."

Scene II

But they all alike began to make excuses. The first said to him, "I have bought a piece of land, and I must go out and see it; please accept my regrets." Another said, "I have bought five yokes of oxen, and I am going to try them out; please accept my regrets." Another said, "I have just been married, and therefore I cannot come." So the slave returned and reported this to his master.

Scene III

Then the owner of the house became angry and said to his slave, "Go out at once into the streets and lanes of the town and bring in the poor, the crippled, the blind, and the lame." And the slave said, "Sir, what you ordered has been done, and there is still room." Then the master said to the slave, "Go out into the roads and lanes, and compel people to come in, so that my house may be filled."

(Luke 14:16b–23 NRSV)

INTRODUCTION

The parable of the poor and the householder contrasts in an important way with the eight other narrative parables studied in this book. The latter start in the present and beckon listeners to consider formative events in the past. In contrast, this parable, which also begins in the present, calls upon listeners to envisage an uncertain future. That course of inquiry is regularly impeded by the allegorical interpretation usually given the parable: the friends who reject the dinner invitation are seen to represent Jewish resistance to Jesus' announcement of the imminent coming of the kingdom of God. The householder, for his part, is said to represent God's welcoming generosity to all those who would enter into the kingdom.

What if the slipper does not fit the foot? The householder's generosity results from his wounded pride. If Jesus were creating an allegory about God providing a great banquet at the end of the age, why would he build it on such a weak foundation? A similar question could be asked about the parable of the prodigal son, which is understood to be a metaphor for God's forgiving love. That interpretation also rests on the strikingly inadequate foundation of a father's inappropriate generosity to an immature son. Both openings suggest that the allegorical approach will not fit. Both are so remarkably perplexing as to invite careful reexamination.

Taking quite a different approach, one could read these narratives as moving, in stages, from possibility, to prediction, to coming into being. Each stage is necessary. One must first imagine the possibility. Next, one must articulate the concept in such a way as to situate it in reality. Then the narrator must shape it into a sequence with a beginning, a middle, and an end. Although every stage will only approximate what is really going on and thus will be incomplete, each will, at the same time, contain some essential part of the whole. Careful exploration of these various stages is key to fully interpreting the parable. The question for the interpreter is: How much of the potential, for good or ill, has the parable disclosed, and how much has it left open-ended?

Parables vary in the degree to which they are filled out. None is a complete story, but some are further along than others. The parable of the poor and a householder has barely begun. Of all the parables in this book, it is the least fully developed.

This parable's central metaphor is a full table. Here the metaphor is clear: there is enough for everyone, including the poor. What is not clear is the householder's motivation. Is the generous offer of a full table intended merely to benefit himself? That is, having been publicly shamed, is he demonstrating to the world that his honor is being restored? If so, the poor have no role to play. They are merely window dressing for the householder's intent to reestablish his position.

Here we encounter an approximation that may be inaccurate but may still contain some essential truth: even if the householder is motivated by more than simply rescuing his honor, the poor can still conclude that his motivation is self-centered. The poor have a history of being abused. They can be skeptical about relying on the promises of the rich. The story then opens up a large potential for mistrust. (Such a reading takes seriously the curious and highly unusual rationale proposed by the parable for the householder's generosity—bring in the poor, the crippled, the blind, and the lame.)

THE HOUSEHOLDER

When the householder invited his friends to his "great dinner," he was hoping they would honor him by accepting his invitation. Yet when his slave says to prospective guests, "'Come, for everything is ready,' . . . they all alike began to make excuses."[1] Here one can understand Jesus to be alluding to the resistance to his message by the well-heeled of his time. As allegory, the refusal by those invited first also fits well with the later church's perception that Jewish Christians who are less well-placed socially, even poor, are superseding recalcitrant Jews. That perception also resonates with Jesus' own dictum, "Blessed are the poor, for they shall inherit the Kingdom of God" (Matt 5:3 NRSV). Yet the listener must still wonder, when supposing Jesus was indeed describing the inexhaustible generosity of his God, why he would choose the wounding of the householder's pride as the reason for it.

We are presented with a carefully structured sequence. (1) The householder has been unexpectedly denied the accepted terms of social prestige, namely, respect from his peers. It is not difficult to imagine the man's hurt at being so roundly rejected. His response to being shamed is so intense it drives him to act impulsively. (2) Only then (and not before) does he decide to be generous to "the poor, the crippled, the blind, and the lame."

It may seem minor at first reading but, as its fundamental premise, the parable posits a sudden, incongruous crossing of a major social boundary. The narrative has a wealthy man doing something no one of his standing ever does: he invites the poor of the street into his home. Eating with others is both an act of intimacy and one that requires reciprocity. Above all, it is an act limited to social equals. When he takes the poor off the street into his home, the householder is violating a firmly established custom, namely, that one dines only with one's equals. But, because many hear this parable as an allegory describing the endless beneficence of a loving God, this highly unusual gesture escapes scrutiny. That way of hearing assumes that the householder's motivation is straightforward and sustainable.

However, if one does not detour into allegory, then one is free to probe the nature of the householder's motivation. The parable goes out of its way to emphasize that the householder becomes generous only in reaction to the earlier rejection. All of his friends with one voice have rebuffed his hospitality. He feels publicly shamed. On the rebound, as it were, he makes an impulsive decision. He invites new guests, all strangers, not of his social class, into his home. Would he have been so generous to the poor had he not been rebuffed by his friends?

---

1. A source for the excuses in the parable, especially for the version in Thomas 64, may have been Deuteronomy 20:5–7, where a priest is addressing troops preparing for battle. "Has anyone built a new house? He should go. Has anyone planted a vineyard? He should go. Has anyone become engaged to a woman and not yet married her? He should go."

Jesus' Parables Speak to Power and Greed

One clue to his state of mind is his shift from inviting to demanding. Here he appears bent on mitigating the humiliation inflicted by his friends. That he commandeers later guests suggests that the rejection by those friends he had invited earlier still stings. The fact that he resorts to imperatives betrays a determined effort to regain his lost respect. It is as if he is saying to his friends, "There! Take that! I am not such an inadequate host as you all think."

Given this unpromising beginning, how likely is it that the householder will be able to sustain his initiative? What will he do with these newfound strangers in his home? Having taken them in, does he have any ambition to engage them further? Or was his remarkable crossing of this boundary occasioned merely by his desire for the respect of new guests to overcome the rejection of the former? Does the presence of the poor in his home serve their needs or his?

The householder's responsiveness to the poor may have come too late. Will he succeed merely in releasing their suppressed resentment towards the longstanding oppression of the householder's class—a resentment he is unlikely to be able to withstand without striking back? The parable uses the householder's wounded pride to draw these two groups into an embrace that has little chance of enduring. Readers may disagree with this perspective, but it offers an opportunity to wonder where in the sequence of historical events there might have been a better chance to succeed.

The parable becomes almost humorous in its suggestion of an abrupt moment of truth. Imagine that the householder suddenly realizes he has invited in the wrong crowd. "Oh my God, what have I done?! What am I doing with these people?" Never before has he been in such close proximity. Where, in the course of this unplanned initiative, does the householder situate himself? Does he watch from the doorway as his slaves serve the meal? Does he sequester himself in his own quarters? Does he take his place at table *with* his guests?

Further questions emerge, both for the householder and the listener. Is the former's wounded honor the only impulse underlying his generosity? Is there any chance he might open up to the experience of these strangers? How far into this unexpected initiative is the householder willing to go? For how long will he tolerate the out-of-place poor occupying the very center of his place in society? For an evening? For a day? Does he say to them the next morning, like a man after a one-night stand, "Well, goodbye. Good luck?" What if he allows his alien guests to stay a week? A month? With what consequences? These questions are not about being right or wrong. They are about whether the householder has sufficient stamina to move beyond an initial but insubstantial investment to discover a truly creative, life-changing interaction.

How, if at all, will the householder's gesture effect significant change? *It turns out that such a decision is up to the listener.* Only if one seriously challenges established social boundaries will one's actions have significant consequences, both "good" and "bad." Just as in the case of the Samaritan rescuing the despised Jew, here the listener is invited to imagine how this initial contact might be carried forward into a sustained relationship. Otherwise both stories are nothing more than simple example stories or divinely engineered allegories.

The question about how long this generous man can maintain the promising initiative he has entered into, for the wrong reasons, is left to the listener's imagination. He had hoped his generosity would coerce respect "on the quick." He was understandably relying on the model used by his peers. You gain respect by giving respect to others. With this suddenly achieved intimacy, he now confronts a central error to which powerful people are prone: "I can't be bothered to earn your respect. I can *make* you be responsive by being generous."

At this point readers might protest. "You are being far too imaginative. The present parable is trying to make a single point: it is about *God's* generosity."

Is it? Who decides? A better question might be: What is the effect of your interpretive decision? To limit the narrative to "one point" places a "No Trespassing" sign on any path to further exploration. Does Jesus participate in such a prohibition? It would appear that, in contrast to later gospel editors, his refusal to explain (and thus place boundaries around) his parables means that there are no right or wrong answers, no restrictions on inquiry, only more or less difficult, more or less interesting pathways to take.

A full table can signify a "full" clientele unexpectedly but momentarily satisfied. Now the story can move from a certain past (restoration of the householder's public honor) through an unstable present (temporarily satisfied) to an uncertain future (satisfied for how long?). Now the context of a "full table" stretches out indefinitely. Is a full table for the poor structured so as to be refilled over time? How full? For how long? Who will maintain it?

The metaphor "full table" embodies a constant act of emptying and refilling. It touches not only on the functioning of bodies but also on the functioning of social structures. Will the poor be included or will they find themselves sidelined once more? The latter—sidelining the poor—is, of course, the age-old response of the rich when facing a conflict between making more money or providing a full table. They may pay lip service to an intervening God. They sometimes invoke charity or foreign aid to muffle the blow. But a substantial reorganization of wealth is nowhere in the cards. In the real world, a table structured to be refilled over time exists only for the wealthy. For everyone else, it must be willed into being. And, as everyone acknowledges, "That will never happen!"

Now imagine for a moment that listeners were to entertain the possibility that the householder's initiative could change him and the future. They could begin to see the different ways in which his generous impulse will be subject to the unexpected consequences that invariably accompany perseverance. If the householder's gesture were to be maintained into some kind of extended future, the implications would become substantial. What continues to nag is the question of whether the householder's motive for being generous will be resilient enough to become a lasting impetus for change. Let's examine the effects of such sustained contact, first on the householder, and then on the poor.

WHAT MIGHT HAPPEN IF THE HOUSEHOLDER SUSTAINS CONTACT WITH THE POOR

A potential for unusual interaction is kindled when the householder invites the poor off the street into his home. By initiating contact across social boundaries, he invites scrutiny of all those social conventions put in place to protect the wealthy from experiencing the suffering of the poor. Wealth notoriously creates distance. Even to mention the word "suffering" would be in poor taste.

Then the parable begins to turn ironic. The householder began his initiative in order to regain respect. But can he gain that respect from people he himself has not yet learned to respect? Can he achieve his goal without first transforming himself? The very act of obliging these dispossessed persons to cross over to him calls the question of whether he should cross over to them. It confronts him with an opportunity to do the hard work of gaining the respect of others by *first* discovering how to give respect to others.

WHAT MIGHT HAPPEN IF THE POOR SUSTAIN CONTACT WITH THE HOUSEHOLDER

These poor suddenly find themselves on the other side of a heretofore unbridgeable chasm, one enforced by the economic and social barriers put in place by the aristocracy. Never before have they been inside the householder's "place." Never before have they had access to evidence of wealth. Never before have they come within speaking distance of the elite. If the householder were to create a safe space for them to express their true feelings, what would inevitably follow would first involve the awareness, and then the expression, of anger. That, in turn, would complicate further interaction (as is the case with any one of the plethora of groups, coalescing in today's identity politics, that ultimately recovers its voice). If the householder cannot tolerate that voice, the potential from his germinal initiative will be lost.

The thing plays out in the listener's imagination. How long will these guests maintain a grateful façade before being emboldened, by the respect from their superior, to express their suppressed feelings of rage and disrespect? ("If you are willing to stay with us long enough, we will make you feel what you have, for so long, made us feel.") The longer the householder sustains his relationship with these unequal poor, the more conflicted his relationship with them will appear—although in fact it more closely resembles the necessary pain accompanying a foot thawing from frost. Will his anger at his earlier humiliation be sufficient to sustain him when his generosity awakens these true, valuable, and potentially restorative manifestations of similar anger?

In parallel fashion, as the poor begin to find their voice, how will that affect the householder's slaves? As they serve their master's food to the poor, what are they thinking? "They're hungry; I'm not." "They're free; I'm not." Along with himself, the householder has propelled both fed and unfed, slave and free into an uncharted space. Impulsively and generously, he has opened up a Pandora's box. The longer these kinds of discord persist, the more untenable they will become. At the same time, however, the longer these interactions carry on, the more authentic their possibilities become. Overlord and underling have together stumbled into conflicts which will either transform them or force them to retreat. For how long will this householder—along with impoverished guests, proud slaves, and parable-listeners—be willing to endure these tensions? For an evening? A week? A month?

Where is the storyteller's God in all this? I would propose that the God of Jesus sits *alongside* the householder, the slaves, the poor, and the story's listeners, as they struggle to take advantage of the householder's remarkable initiative.

INTERWEAVING THE PARABLE WITH MODERN DENIAL

Nowhere else in the parable corpus has the barrier between "above" and "below" been so completely breached. Nowhere has the potential interaction from above and below been so fraught with volatile but promising possibility. It is incumbent upon the listener to sustain the tension and to struggle with the opportunity. "Above" and "below" translate readily into "haves" and "have-nots." Climate denial is authored by the elite among the "haves" and imposed on the "have-nots." If the "have-nots" are complicit in the denial, they are more likely responding to immediate grievances that outweigh the facts about some distant danger. The "haves" must comprehend and acknowledge these grievances before any possibility emerges for the "have-nots" to embrace the danger. Like the householder, we must recover respect for them before there is any chance they will respect our concerns.

The effects of climate breakdown will first of all be visited on the poorest nations and the poorest segments of wealthier nations. Those of us in richer nations have far greater ability to commandeer diminishing resources. Protected by social and economic distance from these multitudes of impersonal poor, we are buffered from direct experience of their despair and their rage. Because we assume we will be insulated from the consequences, we have few incentives to acknowledge their more immediate distress. We tend to dismiss their plight, but it should provoke urgent anxiety, for we are next in line.

Beyond the present rich/poor divide lies a second dimension of distancing that we are even less inclined to acknowledge. Climate breakdown will result in enormous suffering for the vast majority of human beings born three or four generations hence. Despite current debates over the rights of the fetus, no mechanisms have yet been put in place to protect the rights of unborn humans. How will future generations respond to the catastrophic self-centeredness of our own—the last generation able to make any significant difference, the final generation standing between themselves and irreversible tipping points? How will our children's children's children remember what we did not do? Those of us here today have great difficulty imagining the dimensions of their future distress. We have emphatically not welcomed these voices into our consciousness.

This parable points to the wondrous conceit of the rich of the world having to invite millions of future climate refugees into our homes—or at least into our backyards. The alternative will be to push them, through armed resistance, back behind our barriers. But what is in fact a coming reality is, for the moment, mostly relegated to the imagination. Do we *want* to relinquish these barriers of distance that so protect us? How long would we be able to tolerate the immediacy of contact, like that inadvertently provoked by the householder? Would we choose, even in our imagination, to confront the same dilemmas which he has accidentally let pervade his awareness? Once having engaged the have-nots, once having confronted and felt their feelings, once having become conscious of the ways in which we may bear some responsibility for their distress, extracting ourselves will be far more difficult than resorting to our earlier strategy of simply passing by. This parable invites us to share with the householder an intimate experience of ambivalence. It leaves us, sadly, with greater appreciation of why we prefer the comfort of our own denial. It leaves us with the troubling possibility that, in order to survive, we will have to suppress our remaining capacities for fellow feeling.

How much of the householder's focus is on his own well-being and how much on his obligation to those affected by his decisions? How much of his generosity is directed by his challenged sense of honor and how much by his concern for others? The question is not about what is morally right or wrong; it is about identifying which behavior has a chance of effecting a positive difference in history. In the first part of the twenty-first century, the temptation to put today's self-interest before tomorrow's common good is, as always, not immediately countered by emerging reality. That fact that oncoming probabilities do not as yet hurt enough, cost enough, or threaten enough, fuels the denial of climate breakdown. In this parable Jesus does not confront us with accomplished facts; rather, he lures us to anticipate coming possibilities. We can engage them or not, as we will.

Jesus' Parables Speak to Power and Greed

CONTEMPORARY APPLICATIONS

Now that the problem of too much carbon in the atmosphere is acknowledged as global in scope and requiring a global solution, now that countries realize that they cannot solve the issue by acting alone, poor nations and rich nations find themselves unexpectedly occupying the same house. For the first time in history, nations across the earth must either work together or fail together. The old paradigm of "to the victor belongs the spoils" is not only outmoded but lethal. If that paradigm holds, the approaching fate of poor nations will merely serve as advance notice of the eventual fate of our own. While the householder could eject his newfound guests, rich countries cannot do the same to poor nations.

Since we inhabit the same space, poor nations look to rich nations to subsidize their economic development. Put differently, poor nations are not willing to pay the price for the prior success of rich nations. Here it is crucial to recognize that the problem of maintaining a healthy atmosphere is no different than that of maintaining a full table. Both turn on the redistribution of wealth. The resistance to sharing in the vicissitudes of history is the second of two major stumbling blocks to the resolution of climate change. The first, taken up in chapter 3, is the resistance to abandoning the dominant profit motive.

The approaching climate breakdown forces nations into an uncomfortable collaboration. Like an attack by aliens from outer space, climate change obliges everyone to focus on shared goals. However, the disparities in economic resources, as well as the history of their development, give rise to inevitable tensions. Among the leaders struggling with climate change negotiations, the debate is no longer about whether we must all pay. That issue has been settled for some time. Instead, in an effort extending over precious decades, leaders struggle with issues exacerbated by the maldistribution of global wealth. These disparities play out in time-consuming efforts to foist the costs of climate change onto someone else.

Negotiators are caught between a rock and a hard place. Everyone knows that prolonging these tensions increases the cost of the bailout. But no one is accustomed to having the implacable forces of nature arm-twist their national sovereignty. This utterly unified opponent is altogether novel. So, everyone responds by pointing out what others are failing to do. At the same time, however, it is profoundly refreshing to see these issues become the object of active problem-solving rather than being insistently ignored.

It is far more reassuring to confront realistic differences than remain mired in an impasse engineered by the collusion of power and denial.

Frank Ackerman[2] provides one model for resolving the tensions aroused in the quest for an international climate agreement. Two of the major questions under debate are: (a) Who should pay, and (b) what should be a fair distribution of that payment? BAK's model (see the note), which Ackerman adopts, proposes that (1) the right to prior economic development should exempt those persons in each country that falls below a global poverty line from sharing in the costs of ameliorating climate change; (2) any income above that level contributes to each country's share of the global *capacity* to pay for carbon reduction; (3) in turn, each country's *responsibility* to pay is based on its cumulative emissions since 1990 (because by then it was well known that greenhouse gas emissions were contributing to climate breakdown); and (4) from these considerations a cost-sharing formula is created, composed of a weighted average of capacity and responsibility, giving greater weight to capacity.

The householder is subject to none of the urgency that impacts modern climate change-deniers. The latent anger of the oppressed that is poised to upset his intent to be beneficent is still only in the stage of possibility. Just as the householder is unable to foresee his vulnerability, so we have yet to apprehend the elusive evidence of the paradox confronting us: to hold on is to lose; to let go is to gain. Unfortunately, those in positions to make the most significant difference by letting go are the very same people who achieved dominance through the most insistent grasping. Nonetheless, the requirements of climate change now correspond to the requirements of evolution itself. Those fittest to survive are not the ones with the most armaments or the greatest market share; the fittest are those willing to do the "unmanly" work of sharing resources and embracing conservation. In the paradox of the parable, the most promising route open to the householder is to include the poor within the framework of his "home." In the purview of human evolution, "America first" means "America last." In today's world, altruism has become the most potent form of self-interest. It is in fact the most productive, the only, pathway to survival.

---

2. *Can We Afford the Future?* 105–6, summarizing the work of Paul Baer, Thomas Athanasiou, and Sivan Kartha (BAK for short), *Right to Development*.

8

Laborers and a Vineyard Owner
(The Vineyard Workers)

The Situation

A landowner went out early in the morning to hire laborers for his vineyard.

Scene I

After agreeing with the laborers for the usual daily wage, he sent them into his vineyard. When he went out about nine o'clock, he saw others standing idle in the marketplace; and he said to them, "You also go into the vineyard, and I will pay you whatever is right." So they went. When he went out again about noon and about three o'clock, he did the same. And about five o'clock he went out and found others standing around; and he said to them, "Why are you standing here idle all day?" They said to him, "Because no one has hired us." He said to them, "You also go into the vineyard."

Scene II

When evening came, the owner of the vineyard said to his manager, "Call the laborers and give them their pay, beginning with the last and going to the first." When those hired about five o'clock came, each of them received the usual daily wage. Now when the first came, they thought they would receive more; but each of them also received the usual daily wage.

Scene III

And when they received it, they grumbled against the landowner, saying, "These last worked only one hour, and you have made them equal to us who have borne the burden of the day and the scorching heat." But he replied to one of them, "Friend, I am doing you no wrong; did you not agree with me for the usual daily wage? Take what belongs to you and go; I choose to give to this last the same as I give to you. Am I not allowed to do what I choose with what belongs to me? Or are you envious because I am generous?"

(Matthew 20:1–15 NRSV)

Our strategy for approaching these stories remains consistent. We enter from "below," focusing on the particular ways the subordinates are constrained by the overarching dominance of their superior. Then we proceed from "above." We notice how the subordinates' angry response gives their superior an excuse for his self-justification.

THE LABORERS

Because the labor market is flooded, the vineyard workers are in no position to bargain, much less protest, the owner's imposition of an inadequate wage. Partly because of his generosity, but mainly because he controls their survival, the workers fail to see that the source of their distress is the owner's greed. Instead, they accept their less-than-subsistence wages as normal. Their potential for rage is limited to ineffective grumbling about fairness.

They cannot conceive of a larger frame of economic justice. Thus, they cannot muster the resources to appeal to it. They are subject to the owner's whims. Like siblings with negligent parents, they are reduced to fighting with one another. They locate the source of their humiliation in the owner's unfairness, rather than his lawlessness. Though a few workers might be temporarily grateful, their appreciation will soon be overridden by the reality of their chronic deprivation.

THE OWNER

With this short-lived display of charity, the owner is attempting to pass exploitation off as rectitude. But his behavior is not devoted to the welfare of others. He creates this fleeting mini-drama in order to boost his own self-esteem. As his behavior is entirely self-centered, it is difficult to say whether or not he actually believes he is pleasing his workers. He dispenses his generosity though an unjust distribution of rewards. Predictably, the fact that his rewards are disproportionate angers his workmen, as it would any child in any classroom anywhere in the world. "He turned his paper in late. He hardly did any work. And you gave him an A?!" Is it the owner's intent to demean his workers?

Consider the degree of self-deception necessary for the owner to describe himself as "generous." His capacity for charity is, in fact, funded by profits he realizes from paying *all* of his workers too little. By choosing to reward the work of some over others, he further undermines the value of *everyone's* labor. He steals the sense of worth from some in order to foster a fleeting sense of worth in others. "I can inflate or demean the value of your work, as I wish." He thereby packages his claim to generosity in shame. When the drama ends, he will revert to paying a nonliving wage.

Surely the owner's short-term generosity is insufficient to compensate for his long-term payment of inadequate wages. Nonetheless, in spite of his systematic avarice, the owner manifests a certain eagerness to be seen as a good person. But, as his effort is inelegant and self-righteous, the parable almost chokes on it. The owner is so full of himself he invites contempt. He will not even contemplate the legitimacy of the workers' complaint, namely, "You have devalued the only thing I own, the worth of my labor."

The vineyard owner is not being coerced from the outside. No one is making him try to appear generous. Rather he wants to look good. He is troubled enough to create this drama but not enough to take substantive action. His ambivalence results in the humiliation of his workers. He is revealed as someone who is concerned only for his own reputation. Meanwhile, his workers are left on the sidelines helplessly grinding their teeth.

The difference here between appearance and reality is huge: the owner is in fact *not* being generous. As soon as the drama has ended, he will revert to handing out the minimum wage, all the time aware that, for a seasonal agricultural worker subjected to sporadic employment, a denarius a day would not sustain life. The only person in the story deceived by the owner's generosity is the owner himself. To a man, the workers are insulted. Even the lucky ones will side with their grumbling fellows.

That the owner is convinced that he is a good man is striking. The workers' pinpoint critique bounces off him like an arrow off armor. Because it fits so well with his economic interests, his sop is a sufficient balm for his self-esteem. But an instant of generosity is nothing compared to a wholesale overhaul of the wage scale—not to mention thereby taking on the entire agricultural aristocracy. It may mollify some, it may not. But compared to the costs of substantive intervention, such charity is cheap.

THE LISTENER

To arrive at this point, listeners have to set aside the reigning, allegorical interpretation of this story, that is, that the late-coming vineyard workers represent Christians coming late to the kingdom of God. Once that is accomplished, listeners can appreciate how well the story interweaves self-justification with humiliation.

This parable pins the listener between stark alternatives. On the one hand, it can be seen as a story of generosity leading to gratitude. On the other, it recounts a story of calculated disrespect leading to humiliation. In this latter instance, the owner not only refuses to pay all his workers a living wage, but he creates a drama in which he benefits some by depriving others. For workers, the coin of the realm is their labor. It is the only commodity they own. In order to appear generous, the owner raises or lowers its value at will. Thus, for some, the value of an hour's work is greater than for others. This manipulation betrays no recognition of the true problem: that he pays everyone inadequate wages. Instead, the owner succeeds merely in insulting his workers' dignity by disposing largesse *in a manner over which they have no control*. It is a picture of degradation as the owner remains in complete control. The worker does not even control the value of his own labor. In the final debate between worker and owner, the owner insists on defining what is theirs. He is confident he is in the right. He declares himself the owner of what he pays for. He acknowledges no reciprocal obligation to "pay what is right." It is a one-sided contract.

Imagine the inner attitude one must develop towards one's workers in order to inhabit the owner's camp. Dispense with the question of right or wrong. At the heart of the matter is whether or not one respects the workers. One does not show respect for all of them by rewarding only some of them. The owner could have resolved this problem by giving all of his workers a proportionate bonus, but he did not. That would have required him to value their labor. Rather, he gave those he excluded cause to complain. How does the reader not empathize with those neglected workers? Why does the reader not join in the complaint of those who labored longer? "These last worked only one hour, and you have made them equal to us who have borne the burden of the day and the scorching heat."

At this point, the parable makes a wondrous observation about the price one must pay when importing an intervening God. Parable interpretations that stress the generosity of the vineyard owner as a God figure ignore his reprehensible self-serving. Understanding the owner as a God-figure able to make things right relieves listeners of the difficult work of having to imagine what it is like to be tyrannized, economically deprived, bullied, and systematically excluded from decisions that can be life-threatening.

Most importantly, that interpretation lets readers circumvent the difficult work of imagining what it is like to be silenced. This not only entails being rendered completely voiceless, but it also involves the long-standing, complete censorship of any and all attempts to articulate the problem. The workers who grumble at being denied an anticipated extra reward for a day's labor have no concept of the deeper sources of their humiliation. They lack narratives to be able to explain how the aristocracy, over centuries, has systematically deprived them of a living wage. The listener must work to reconstruct these missing narratives, while at the same time pausing to recognize the exquisite artistry that has deliberately crafted their absence.

MODERN APPLICATIONS

In this reading, the place where parable and contemporary issues resonate is found in the owner's conviction that he has succeeded in looking good, when in fact he has betrayed his workers. While positioning himself as their benefactor, he actually humiliates them. This is possible only because he is oblivious to the realities faced by marginal laborers trying to survive on a less-than-living wage. In today's world, a parallel can be found in the attitude of the Democratic Party which, in recent decades, has convinced itself it can get away with steadily degrading the working class.

Thomas Frank's well-documented book, *Listen, Liberal or Whatever Happened to the Party of the People?* (2016) describes how, beginning particularly with the presidency of Bill Clinton, Democratic policies, especially trade policies like NAFTA, have regularly been inimical to worker interests. This change in the longstanding Democratic position transpired almost unnoticed by the managerial class. Thus, in the 2016 election, nearly everyone was caught off guard by the working-class rush to support Republican candidates. The failure of the vineyard owner to understand the degree of his affront to his workers is mirrored today by the failure of modern interpreters who still identify him as a generous God-figure. Not one worker, not even those who temporarily benefited, would agree. Similarly, the animosity of Democratic workers towards their seemingly beneficent candidates rumbled silently below the surface. It was not a revolution. It was an erosion.

> In this country, from the middle of the Great Depression up to 1980 the lower 90 percent of the population . . . took home some 70 percent of the growth in the country's income. Look at the same numbers beginning in 1997—from the beginning of the New economy—and you find that this same group of American people, pocketed none of American's income growth at all. Their share of the good times was zero. The gains they harvested after all their hard work were nil. The upper 10 percent of the population—the country's financiers, managers, and professionals—ate the whole thing. The privileged are doing better than at any time since economic records begin.[1]

The surprise and dismay of Democrats at the outcome of the 2016 presidential election is clear evidence of their miscalculation about the degree of disaffection among working-class voters. The former trusted their own economic security. They failed to take on board the fear and anger engulfing so many Americans. In that sense, they are like the vineyard owner who believed that his staged drama, though lacking any substantial

---

1. Frank, *Listen, Liberal*, 2

Jesus' Parables Speak to Power and Greed

correction of the wage structure, would nonetheless gain the allegiance of his workers.

A similar deception is thriving today.

> The Democrats posture as the "party of the people" even as they dedicate themselves ever more resolutely to serving and glorifying the professional class. Worse: they combine self-righteousness and class privilege in a way that Americans find stomach-turning. And every two years, they simply assume that being non-Republican is sufficient to rally the voters of the nation to their standard . . . [Yet] the Democrats have no interest in reforming themselves in a more egalitarian way.[2]

The parable is a first-rate example of appearance without substance. The initial euphoria that something is finally happening will give way to anger as soon as it becomes clear that, once again, workers have been duped. Just as the short-term gain is predictable, so is the long-term insult. How is it that both the vineyard owner and the modern petroleum oligarch refuse to acknowledge what is coming? Abandon the pretense that they simply do not see it. The fact is they do not want to see what is coming. Why? Because it would cost them—a lot. Just about everything they have. (Of course, it would also make them immoral.) Democratic policies that are antithetical to workers' interests have, not surprisingly, fostered worker indifference to the concerns of the managerial class, particularly with regard to climate change.

One can portray, but not explain, how modern fossil fuel executives can sustain the belief that their public relations campaigns will succeed. As with the vineyard owner, the success of their deceit, coupled with its cover-up, will provoke even more anger and scorn. We are still left trying to understand the mindset of fossil fuel executives who are deliberately planning to burn six times the amount of carbon the earth can absorb.[3] In coming centuries, these leaders will be vilified as murderers. While ostensibly their public relations campaigns are designed to deceive the public, they also are intended to salve their own consciences.

The only solution to this problem—leaving the fuel in the ground—constitutes an invitation to suicide for fossil fuel corporations. The parable brilliantly depicts their fallback position: an impossible contortion that masks exploitation as generosity. Both the owner and the executive are like

---

2. Frank, *Listen, Liberal,* 256.
3. McKibben, "Global Warming's Terrifying New Math."

a child who crawls into an abandoned pipe but can only go so far before becoming stuck, unable to proceed or to extricate himself. Fossil fuel leaders know that burning fossil fuels is deadly. So, they put on a show of creating alternative fuels. This diversion serves their purpose, that is, to ensure that fossil fuels themselves are not impacted. What appears as executive stupidity is, in fact, evidence of an executive impasse. There is no way out. Better to deceive the public and themselves.

British Petroleum's short-lived "green sun" search for alternative fuels is one example. BP did nothing substantive to address the problem. Instead, they devoted their energies *to looking like* they were solving the problem. They created a false narrative to hide a truly dangerous situation. The cover-up itself betrays the degree to which they are aware that they should be doing something far more substantial.

The parable illustrates worker vulnerability. Those of us in blue states are not economically dependent on the oil oligarchs. We can readily oppose their unrestrained pollution. In contrast, Louisiana oil workers are entirely dependent on the oligarchs for their economic security. They cannot react to, much less oppose, the violence to their economic position and physical health. Thus, they excuse the greed of oil oligarchs, "Factories are like people; they have to shit."

Lower-middle-class, white workers are buying into the false promises of far-right politicians because no one else articulates their widespread disappointment. These disaffected middle Americans are overwhelmed by feelings of unfairness and humiliation. They long for political leaders who will passionately voice their resentment. Their denial of climate change is fueled by the perception that they are not being respected. So accustomed are they to lack of respect that they welcome any appearance of regard, as if it were real. Those who are able to work, and are unwilling to go on welfare, are looking for jobs, not charity. But economic pressures are moving jobs overseas. And it is far more difficult to bring to fruition government policies that facilitate growth in well-paying manufacturing jobs than to give federal welfare subsidies. These workers uncritically embrace the pronouncements of politicians who, with seeming sincerity, declare, "I love uneducated people." For their part, the politicians, who are controlled by the oligarchs, betray their followers by manipulating them to put nails in the coffin of climate change. Ironically, it appears that many of the very

Jesus' Parables Speak to Power and Greed

voters who support such politicians come from areas in the U.S. that are the most vulnerable to climate change disaster.[4]

That white, American, blue-collar workers support politicians who in turn support the oligarchs is terrifying. And terror is not conducive to understanding. We find ourselves despising these voters because we fear the consequences of oligarchic control. As a result, our responses become ill-considered. Rather than blaming workers (and the subordinates in the parable), we must try to understand how we have in fact abandoned them to subjugation and disposal by the powerful.

Parable-listeners are initially drawn to side with the story's dominant character, while working-class voters unknowingly side with the oligarchs. Modern middle-class readers, on the other hand, are not nearly as susceptible to the oligarchs' claims to represent them. There is a potential here for joining the parable with the present. Once listeners have stripped the superior of his protective coloring as a God figure (a perception highly unlikely to have been shared by Jesus' original listeners), once they perceive his lack of shame and absence of concern, they will find few reasons to suppose he has the capacity to provide protection or positive change for his victims.

Jesus' parables entice us to unravel the distancing, disguises, and deceptions fashioned over long histories of domination. Using the same strategies, we can reevaluate the history leading up to the now-urgent phenomenon of climate denial. We must challenge the normalization of the distortions that persons in power have always used to mask their true purposes. By realizing how completely we have ceded control of existing definitions to the dominant figure in the parable, we can appreciate how we have allowed powerful climate deniers to inflict a similar sleight of hand on today's public. By discovering the longstanding linkage between the attempts at coercion by the dominant figure and the compromised resistance of the subordinate, we can come closer to understanding what led up to both the engineering of climate doubt and to the public responses of indifference or displaced anger.

---

4. See Joyce, "Mapping the Potential Economic Effects."

9

Jesus' Parable and the Genesis Stories of Two Sons and a Father

The Situation

There was a man who had two sons.

Scene I

The younger of them said to his father, "Father give me the share of the property that will belong to me."

So he divided his property between them.[1]

---

1. Shakespeare has a father respond very differently to his son's desire for premature control over his inheritance. In *King Lear*, Edmund, the illegitimate son, seeks by a ruse to turn his father Gloucester against his brother, the legitimate son Edgar: "I have heard him oft maintain it to be fit that, sons at perfect age and fathers declined, the father should be as ward to the son, and the son manage his revenue." Gloucester responds, "O villain, villain! His very opinion in the letter! Abhorred villain! Unnatural, detested, brutish villain! Worse than brutish! Go, sirrah, seek him; I'll apprehend him. Abominable villain! Where is he?" (*King Lear*, Act I, Scene 2).

Scene II

A few days later the younger son gathered all he had and traveled to a distant country, and there he squandered his property in dissolute living.

When he had spent everything, a severe famine took place throughout that country, and he began to be in need. So he went and hired himself out to one of the citizens of that country, who sent him to his fields to feed the pigs. He would gladly have filled himself with the pods that the pigs were eating; and no one gave him anything.

But when he came to himself he said, "How many of my father's hired hands have bread enough and to spare, but here I am dying of hunger! I will get up and go to my father and I will say to him, 'Father I have sinned against heaven and before you; I am no longer worthy to be called your son; treat me like one of your hired hands.'" So he set off and went to his father.

Scene III

But while he was still far off, his father saw him and was filled with compassion; he ran and put his arms around him and kissed him.

The son said to him, "Father, I have sinned against heaven and before you; I am no longer worthy to be called your son."

But the father said to his slaves, "Quickly, bring out a robe—the best one—and put it on him."

"Put a ring on his finger and sandals on his feet."

"And get the fatted calf and kill it, and let us eat and celebrate; for this son of mine was dead and is alive again; he was lost and is found!" And they began to celebrate.

(Luke 15:11–32 NRSV)

Jesus' Parable and the Genesis Stories of Two Sons and a Father

INTRODUCTION

The story begins with a staggering concurrence between a younger son's grandiose demand for an unearned livelihood and his father's uncritical willingness to provide it. Here one encounters a compelling reference to stories of unearned preference found in Genesis—about Jacob's successful theft of an inheritance and about the adolescent Joseph's sense of preeminence among his siblings. This entire parable can be seen to spell out the consequences of such favoritism. Likewise, at the heart of climate denial is a sense, rife among rich nations, of entitlement. This pairing of the "privileged" younger son and the indulgent father becomes a rich resource for exploring contemporary misperceptions.

We approach this parable from below, that is, from the point of view of the younger son. To grasp his perspective, we need to step back and imagine what this immature young man was up against. His older brother will inherit the land. As a younger son, he lacks access to anything remotely approaching his brother's already established identity. At the same time, as he comes from a well-off family, he is not forced by poverty into a specific, limited role. He does not yet know what he wants to do, what he can do, or how effective he will be at doing it.

The younger son's request captures an exceedingly fraught moment between father and son. By asking for his inheritance before his father has died, the son breaks with all precedents. Why? What is he truly seeking? Is he looking for capitulation or does he want resistance? Does he hope his father will up and die or that he will up and become a father? If the father accedes to his son's insolent request, what message will that send? From his later decisions, it is evident that the son intended to leave home and emigrate to a foreign country. He could have requested a limited gift to support this exploration. But no. The fact that he seeks control over financial resources essential to his father's own well-being reveals a larger, as yet unresolved, desire to establish his independence. We can imagine at least two paternal responses: either his father firmly refuses, or he "generously" agrees. In what follows, the father's "no" would have been a generous "yes." His unfortunate "yes" becomes a tragic "no."

With his unprecedented request, the younger son tempts his needy father into breaking major boundaries. With the father's collusion, the son prematurely procures an inheritance that prevents him from developing his own resources. Missing is a father who confidently expects his son to grow. This parent appears to doubt that his child can survive. In turn, because of his "success," the son becomes susceptible to the belief that he is somehow special, that he deserves what he has received. This presumption not only has the potential to overpower any incentive for him to conserve, but it also stunts his capacity to produce. In despair, he realizes his father has lost confidence in his ability to become a man. At this point he determines to destroy what is, in fact, not his.

By acceding to his son's request, by permitting him to avoid the risks he must take to discover his adult abilities, the father may indeed be telegraphing his fundamental doubt about his son's capability. At the very least, he is evincing a desire to keep his son immature and dependent, thus requiring his son to choose between risky loyalty to his own growth, on the one hand, and dead-end loyalty to his father's need to be needed, on the other.

The hypothesis explored here is that the son does, in fact, not want the inheritance. Rather, he is trying to discover what his father really thinks of his abilities. Can he make it on his own? Above all, can he make it on his own outside his family? Here the father's refusal would signal both awareness that his younger son is not yet ready for such responsibility as well as confidence in his son's ability to grow. By requiring him to stay longer in a family context, the father would have given his son a much greater chance of success. The son's later shame at his inevitable failure may reveal an earlier, if ambivalent, wish that his father had refused him, and thereby demonstrated that he believed that his son would, in time, become equal to those risks. When the son finds himself trapped into leaving home, as though he were already mature, he not only gives up on himself, but he also leaves with the certain knowledge that his father has likewise given up on him.

To go down this path, listeners must take two very large steps: first, relinquish the prevalent idea that the father represents the desire or intention of God (an understanding clearly embedded in the Lukan context for the story); and second, ponder what a story about a breakdown between father and son, leading to an essentially false restitution, could possibly be about.

This story deeply engages with the Genesis accounts of a father and two sons. What does Jesus intend when he so clearly addresses his own tradition? He appears to embrace the dangers of feeling special, of believing oneself preferred. When we are given so much so soon, he seems to ask, are we obliged to give back, or can we assume some entitled right to take?

The parable is a brilliant critique of any claim to divine entitlement that eschews responsibility. It can be read as a metaphor concerning Israel's assumption that, as the chosen people, they can possess the land without reciprocal obligation. It can be seen to be facing in two directions at the same time: then, towards the foundations of Israel; now, towards the uncertain future of the modern world. Both perspectives are threatened by a sense of entitlement. The betrayal inherent in a national identity that assumes the absence of obligation prefigures global assumptions of exclusive ownership that undermine humanity's commitment to reciprocity. The god-figure, represented by the generous father, is diametrically opposed to the God of the universe (that is, the way things function well). What kind of benevolent God, the parable asks, do we choose to worship?

In modern, secular terms, the parable can be seen to challenge the conviction that the natural order has, in fact, ceded the resources of the earth to those who claim to own them. Does nature simply provide without requiring reciprocity? Are we given the world's oil to do with as we wish? Or do the laws of physics exact an inviolable respect for limit? Here the conceit of entitlement wrestles with the realities of responsibility. Relying on one's privilege, climate denial rests on rejecting one's responsibility. Both then and now, if responsibility is ignored, the consequences of choosing to believe in unconditional generosity can be devastating.

THE PARABLE AND ITS GENESIS BACKGROUND

The present chapter offers a departure from generally accepted approaches to this parable. It argues that Jesus entered into a sustained dialogue with revered ancient narratives, found in the book of Genesis, about a father and two sons. Here Jesus interrogates the multiple implications of the Pentateuch's fundamental thesis that God gives the land to Israel.[2] Does God give without condition? What is the relationship between being chosen and being responsible? What consequences are there for those who convert a belief that they are chosen into an assumption that they are privileged? If you assume a gift was given without any corresponding responsibility to the giver, then you may do with it whatever you wish. To appreciate the implications, we turn first to the ways in which this parable may be revisiting the Genesis stories.

2. See Davies, *Territorial Dimension of Judaism*, 13.

Jesus' Parables Speak to Power and Greed

JESUS' PARABLE OF TWO SONS AND A FATHER COMPARED WITH THE GENESIS STORIES OF TWO SONS AND A FATHER

As a basis for comparison, what follows lays out the parable (Luke 15:11b–32 NRSV), interspersed with references from Genesis (translation: *Tanakh, The Holy Scriptures*) in italics, followed by commentary.

The Situation

There was a man who had two sons.

In response to a query from a discomfited Rebekah about why her twins (Esau, i.e., Edom, representing the surrounding tribes in Canaan, and Jacob, i.e., Israel) are wrestling inside her body, the Lord replies, "Two nations are in your womb, two separate peoples shall issue from your body; one people shall be mightier than the other, and the older shall serve the younger" (Gen 25:23).

In this story, as in multiple Genesis narratives of a father and two sons (Abraham with Ishmael and Isaac; Isaac with Esau and Jacob; and Jacob with Joseph and his brothers), God chooses the younger son (Israel) to receive the inheritance (the land). He denies the inheritance to the elder son (the competing tribes also living in Canaan). (In giving the inheritance of the land to their younger sons, these fathers break God's law. [Deut 21:15–17].) Recipients are thereafter forever poised between grateful awe at the opportunity to represent God's purposes in the world and the assumption of privilege that entitles them to take from others. This tension takes many forms and passes through many permutations.

Scene I

The younger of them said to his father, "Father give me the share of the property that will belong to me."

> *God is speaking to Abraham: "I assign the land you sojourn in to you and your offspring to come, all the land of Canaan, as an everlasting holding"* (Gen 17:8).
>
> *Jacob demands of Esau: "... sell me your birthright.... So [Esau] ... swore to him, and sold his birthright to Jacob"* (Gen 25:31, 33).
>
> *"Israel [Jacob] loved Joseph best of all his sons, for he was the child of his old age; and he made him an ornamented tunic. And when his brothers saw that their father loved him more than any of his brothers, they hated him"* (Gen 37:3–4).

So he divided his property between them.

One prototype for the father in Jesus' parable is almost certainly the doting father Jacob, who at this particular moment in the Genesis story becomes a caricature of a parent who favors one child over others. With immense irony, by favoring his adolescent son Joseph, this father needlessly provokes the envy of Joseph's elder brothers, thereby endangering the very son he loves most. With amazing obtuseness, Jacob repeats an earlier pattern that nearly cost him his life. By enacting this preference, he exposes his own younger son to the same lethal danger which his mother, in collusion with God, visited on him. By so clearly alluding to repeated Genesis themes of parents provoking disaster, the parable alerts its well-versed listeners to the deeper sources of its tragedy.

Scene II

A few days later the younger son gathered all he had and traveled to a distant country *[a hint at Abraham's Canaan]*, and there he squandered his property in dissolute living.

At this early stage, the parable is exploring the burden put upon the younger son by his father's premature generosity. The inheritance is a concentrated form of sudden wealth, unearned and undeserved, representing the work of previous generations. By handing it over prematurely, the father undermines his son's nascent sense of competence. The father's "gift," while seemingly directed at establishing his son's autonomy, in fact undermines it. At this point of unrelieved self-deception, the son genuinely believes he deserves his father's largesse.

The prodigal possesses his fortune the same way his father possesses him. Each has learned that the other's provision is there for the taking. The father does not want his son to be able to separate from his cloying "love." The son relies on his father's need to be needed to leverage the inheritance. The son suffers from a successful taking that involves no obligation. Instead of developing the capacity to survive on his own, he learns to rely on what his father is all too ready to give. (These are all descriptions of the kind of god the privileged worshiper chooses to believe in.) His success in manipulating his father undermines his ability to develop the capacity he needs to separate from him. What little autonomy he does exhibit does not equip him with what he needs. He is instead reduced to buying admiration and acceptance that he cannot otherwise earn. By being the sole author of his son's seeming competencies, the father sends his son into the world in a manner precisely designed to eventuate in his defeat.

The son may not have truly wanted the inheritance. Somehow, he has been dimly sensing that his father was preventing his growth and keeping him immature by virtue of a possessive love. That he prematurely asks for possession of his father's resources may reveal an unconscious attempt to probe his father's limits. He was seeking assurance that his father would insist on maintaining control of the resources in order to complete his own work, thus revealing the father's confidence that the son will in time accomplish the work that falls to him. The son's seemingly hurtful demand, that his father behave as though he were dead, may in fact represent the son's ambivalent hope that his parent might come alive, reveal himself as a father, and assume the authority that for a long time has been lacking. His provocation may be a last-ditch effort to discover the boundaries essential for his own growth. (Here is a framing of the modern despair that arises from humanity's inability to establish the limits of the earth requisite for sustainable growth.)

The son is left with no choice but to leave home. However, when reaching his destination, he is altogether unprepared for his next steps. In fact, he faces a checkmate. The burden of his father's provision has prevented him from developing his own resources. Trapped in a perverse sense of entitlement, he has eventually to conclude that he is who he is only because of what he has been given. His seemingly reprehensible profligacy represents a necessary jettisoning of a useless paternal resource. His squandering of his father's provision mirrors his father's squandering of his place as father. Unwilling to return to a home where he cannot grow, his only option is to regress to a state where he is forced to return. (Here in the absence of authoritative limits, is a model for the reckless position of the modern fossil fuel industry and the larger society along with it. Because it cannot develop a sustainable future, it will revert to eating its base.)

In this reading, the parable is examining the particular threat facing those who understand themselves to be divinely chosen. The problem is emphatically not that of being specially selected. That opens the potential for all kinds of responsible realizations of divine purpose. Rather, the problem is that of mistaking that selection for a deserved privilege. At the heart of climate denial is the conviction found among the rich nations of the world that they deserve the right to waste the lion's share of the earth's resources.

> When he had spent everything, a severe famine took place throughout that country, and he began to be in need. So he went and hired himself out to one of the citizens of that country, who sent him to his fields to feed the pigs. He would gladly have filled himself with the pods that the pigs were eating; and no one gave him anything.
>
> But when he came to himself he said, "How many of my father's hired hands have bread enough and to spare, but here I am dying of hunger! I will get up and go to my father and I will say to him, 'Father I have sinned against heaven and before you; I am no longer worthy to be called your son; treat me like one of your hired hands.'" So he set off and went to his father.

It is important to note how at the nadir of his experience the son is able to articulate what he needs most: responsible work within authoritative limits. That this father will have none of it serves to underscore the story's larger irony: that an overgenerous god-figure is responsible for the son's inability to thrive.

Scene III

> But while he was still far off, his father saw him and was filled with compassion; he ran and put his arms around him and kissed him.

> *Joseph, the younger son, vice-regent of all Egypt, rushes to meet his long-lost father, falls on his neck, and weeps. (Gen 46:29)*

The son said to him, "Father, I have sinned against heaven and before you; I am no longer worthy to be called your son."

> *When the humiliated son tries to speak, his words are far from any the victorious younger son Joseph might utter. With hunger-fighting shame, he confesses, "I have sinned against heaven and before you." These words are lifted from the lips of the most powerful man in the world. The younger son's speech echoes the confession of the defeated Pharaoh who, after resisting the divine impact of seven plagues upon himself and his people, is finally brought to his knees by the eighth. "Pharaoh hurriedly summoned Moses and Aaron and said, 'I stand guilty before the Lord your God and before you'" (Exod 10:16).[3] Along with Pharaoh, one can see the son here either as insincere or as sincerely defeated by a force beyond his control.*

But the father said to his slaves, "Quickly, bring out a robe—the best one—and put it on him."

> *Israel [Jacob] loved Joseph best of all his sons, for he was the child of his old age; and he had made him an ornamented tunic. (Gen 37:3)*

"Put a ring on his finger and sandals on his feet."

> *Removing his signet ring from his hand, Pharaoh put it on Joseph's hand; he arrayed him in garments of fine linen . . . (Gen 41:42)*

And get the fatted calf and kill it, and let us eat and celebrate; for this son of mine was dead and is alive again; he was lost and is found!" And they began to celebrate.

In a comparison of the Joseph saga with the parable, a consistent coupling of opposites between Joseph and the prodigal son stands out. The trajectory of the parable runs exactly opposite to the trajectory of the Joseph saga. In his story, Joseph, a younger son in a distant country, moves from

---

3. I owe awareness of this textual parallel to Bailey, *Jacob and the Prodigal*, 106.

enslavement to a position of great wealth. In the parable, the younger son in a distant country moves from wealth to virtual enslavement. Joseph's rise to power is marked by intense probity and good judgment. The younger son seems motivated by an equally focused effort to fail. Joseph, anticipating the worldwide famine to come, stores the produce of all Egypt in vast warehouses. The younger son, lacking even the capacity to anticipate his own hunger, flings his patrimony to the winds. In the center of his story, Joseph—under contract to serve a gentile—is discovered as supremely confident, superbly competent, and engaged in feeding the entire world. In the center of his story, the younger son—under contract to serve a gentile—is found defeated, resourceless, and unable to feed even himself. Joseph is protected by the story's logic from suffering any of the untoward effects of being preferred. Enveloped in God's purpose, he slips by without consequence into the most comprehensive of adult competencies. That he consistently lands on his feet becomes oppressively unrealistic. No individual or nation can be that persistently successful. By contrast, the parable holds its listeners within the far more constricted domain of a doting father and a weakly developed son. Only later will the parallels again converge when the reckoning of ancient Israel takes place first within centuries of slavery, and then across forty years wandering in the wilderness.

During his self-defeating odyssey, also ending in slavery, the son has begun to realize that only by working within limits can he become a man. But he has as yet only a weak understanding of how his father's generosity is undermining his need to take responsibility. Once reunited with his father, he tries and fails to be reinstated, not as a privileged son but rather as a responsible worker. But he can only think it; he cannot get the words out. "For God's sake, treat me like one of your hired hands." The father is oblivious to his son's need. As he rushes to embrace his long-lost child, he tramples on this glowing ember of hope. The son's fragile plea is silenced. His humiliation is so overwhelming that he cannot conceive of challenging his father's obtuseness. Instead, he attacks himself. The parable leaves him there, in the grip of a prolonged sense of shame.

The parable leverages its complex allusions to the ways in which the possession of privilege introduces loss from Genesis. Throughout the sagas of Jacob and Esau and of Joseph and his brothers, Genesis spells out the costs of a father choosing the younger son. For Jacob to possess the blessing, Esau is betrayed. For Israel to possess the land, Edom is conquered. For Jacob to favor Joseph, his brothers are reduced to murder. For Joseph to become a prince, Israel is enslaved. For God to privilege some, others must be excluded.

In this way Genesis exposes at least two major problems lying in wait for those who perceive themselves to be chosen, namely, that (1) those privileged are tempted to believe that they deserve their entitlement, and (2) those not privileged endlessly resent the former's elevation. The parable engages these dangers; it becomes a description of how the father's peremptory bestowal of privilege threatens the development of both his sons.

INTERWEAVING THE PARABLE WITH MODERN DENIAL

In the Genesis stories, the divinely ordained privileging of the younger son over his older siblings can be seen as a way of exposing the privileging of some nations over others. This assumption of privilege is just one component of a whole series of aggrandizing moves justified as normal but which in fact depend on raw force. European immigrants to the New World assumed that their God had gifted them the entire western reach of the North American continent. Settlers went west and appropriated the land and its resources, not because they had the right, but because they could. Their success set the stage for the modern-day acquisition, without constraint, of the oil, gas, and coal deposited underground over millions of years. The enormity of the damage enabled by this exploitation is only now beginning to be felt.

To justify the idea that God has given us this inheritance—this land, this oil—to do with as we wish, we must rely on only one aspect of the myths developed in the ancient Hebrew tradition. By preserving only rights and draining these myths of responsibility, we effect a decisive shift in balance. Here obligation wanes and entitlement thrives. The inheritance now involves no obligation to others. No longer are we required to observe justice; we have merely to assert that we have been divinely chosen. The parable sits at the center of this shift in balance.

The younger son left home thinking he had no work to do. By contrast the elder son, who stayed home, imagines he has too much work to do. He has the misfortune to come up against a father unable to rejoice in his son's growing independence. Locating the problem in himself, he doubles down on hard work in a hopeless effort to break through his father's inability to recognize his competence. Understandably, he becomes ambivalent. He is envious of his brother's manipulation of their needy father but unwilling to sacrifice his own growth. Both sons must eventually embrace the fact that their father cannot cope with them developing independence.

The father is intent on keeping his sons dependent on him. He fails to demonstrate any expectation that either of them will be able to prosper on his own. As he depends on them for his own self-worth, he does not want his sons to discover their worth apart from him. That he controls them through generosity further complicates their efforts to separate from him.

When the father and his sons are reunited, the forces leading to the earlier shaming and resentment are still very much alive. The younger son will have to struggle to avoid being reinstated to privilege, to become a responsible worker able to accept the demands of reality. During his failed odyssey, he did at least discover that he can become a man only by working within limits. The elder son will have to look elsewhere for confirmation of his abilities.

The reader needs to wonder, "How does this younger son's wasting his inheritance seem to him the best decision he can make under the circumstances?" Such questioning is a way to avoid simplistically assigning blame. The younger son has had the misfortune of successfully manipulating his father into giving him what he was not able to earn on his own. A number of interpretations propose that in his later extremity "the son was simply looking to be fed and was using his father to this end." The present reading reverses this sequence. Instead, it asserts that, "The father was simply looking to be fed and is using his son to this end."

Because the father so desperately wants his son to continue needing him, he offers him the nurture of childhood rather than the discipline of adolescence. Disguising his control as beneficence, he wields his generosity to cover up his need to be needed. This tempts the younger son into a perverse sense of entitlement. In the end, he reaches the difficult conclusion that he is who he is only because of what he has been given. That leaves him with no recourse but to destroy his false privilege. As he is unable to oppose his father directly, he attacks by collapsing. For this he pays a huge price. His shame drowns out any remaining vestiges of confidence.

The father's gift is to himself. He has sabotaged his son's development. His awareness is clouded by his conscious sense of great love for his son. Had he been confronted with the way in which, by prematurely bestowing the inheritance, he brought about his son's humiliation, he would have been astonished. (Likewise, the doting Jacob would have been astounded to realize that, by foolishly privileging Joseph, he imperiled his beloved son's life.)

Listeners are left trying to understand why the sons of this father, this seeming paragon of a loving parent, feel so unloved. They must consider whether the reasons for the collapse of one son and the rage of the other owes to the father's need to be needed. They must look again at how the wellspring of these sons' development has been compromised. Listeners will be drawn to reevaluate the risks embedded in their own beliefs in being specially chosen. In so doing, they will consider not only the chosen citizens of ancient Israel but also the privileged citizens of America today. By gaining premature possession of the earth's resources, we too are seduced into believing we are actually in control.

MODERN APPLICATIONS

Could this narrative in fact comprise what this reading proposes, namely, a subtle presentation of the dangers confronting those who would worship an all-providing, nondemanding god, a god who selects only them for his special provision? It invites listeners to look again at this father, at this person so convinced of his own effectiveness, so protected by any challenge to his authority, and so revered by centuries of admirers. Although seeming to render him as a figure embodying God's love, the parable instead may be offering listeners a chance to ponder the consequences of entrusting themselves to a god who responds as does this father. Could the theme of being chosen, juxtaposed with the need to squander, be the double-take the parable is reaching for?

The parable, in a modern context, critiques our understanding of the limits of the natural order, our desire for inexpensive energy no matter how dangerous, and our tolerance of the fossil fuel executives who provide it. In this reading, it challenges at least three of our most cherished presumptions, namely, that (1) we possess a God who is unreservedly generous to a select few, (2) our privilege is deserved, and (3) our privilege has no adverse consequences.

The conversation which Jesus was here having with his fellow Jews concerning their sense of being chosen can be readily applied to our own presumption that God has chosen us, our nation, our class. Like the prodigal, we are selected for some special provision of wealth and well-being, while at the same time not held accountable for this favoritism. But what kind of love provides resources without requiring responsibility? What kind of irony is lodged in the idea of loving God, who responds to our immaturity first by dismissing our obligations and then by forgiving our inevitably destructive behavior?

Is our earthly inheritance truly ours to consume without demand for discipline? Or do we merely experience an illusion of ownership? An immature god fathers immature offspring. This religious ideology sanctions an unrestrained desire to take what is not ours. The illusion of owning what we have not earned further leads us to squander what we imagine has no limit. We even believe we have the right to appropriate what belongs to others. In the present reading, this parable becomes a commentary on the extraordinary dangers of believing in a deity who privileges those who worship him.

A parallel presumption can be found in the secular sphere. Those of us who derive benefits from exploiting natural resources assume we do, in fact, own those resources. We convince ourselves that this inheritance is ours to dispose of as we wish. In a brief three-century period of "riotous living," we have depleted a fossil fuel inheritance created over 300 million years. Our conviction that we own what we have been given creates the illusion that we deserve what we have. We even believe that the earth gives us the right to use its resources further to despoil the earth! While we are quick to embrace the narratives of meritocracy, we are even quicker to deny the extent to which our success depends on the gifts of nature.

Fossil fuel executives are happy to fill the role of a prodigal deity. They have consistently devoted their profits to crippling government's ability to regulate them. Asserting that they own what they have not produced, they reject responsibility for the costs of what they have taken. Along with the parable father, these executives foresee no adverse consequences arising from their exercise of largesse. Their distorted sense of privilege results in a distorted sense of entitlement. Ironically, they join the son. Being awash in enormous sums of money (as is the son), these same executives are sucked into a shared delusion. They believe they can control the outcome of their squandering.

Like both prodigal and executive, consumers also believe they have a right to what was never theirs and no responsibility for what they have received. We will continue burning through our carbon reserves no matter what the cost. "Give us our inheritance now, to do with as we wish. Forgo any demand that we demonstrate the capacity to manage these resources on behalf of the planet's future. Drop any expectation that we should place our privilege in the service of those we deprive. And for God's sake, do not keep on warning us that such deluded ambition will bring crashing down upon us extremes of misery and destitution."

The failure of both father and son to anticipate the future is striking. Both restrict their calculations of benefits to the present. There is no opportunity for the son to learn to live within limits. The seemingly endless frontier in the United States provides similar grounds for denying limits.

The parable is wonderfully paced. For every thoughtless denial of limits, it posits a corresponding imposition of limits. If we choose to live for the present over the future, we will follow the father and son into privileging immediate gratification over future survival. The future has no voice in the present. Its only ally is the human ability to anticipate the future. Thus, an articulate fifteen-year-old from Sweden can have enormous influence. In forty-five years, she will be sixty. In forty-five years, she will be experiencing, physically, the consequences of decisions we make today. Either we must accept our limit, or she will be forced to live with the effects of our refusal. And she knows it.

Why do listeners overlook the devastating failure of the father to impose limits on the son's demand for immediate, unearned gratification? Doing so lands them in precisely the same box as those seeking immediate gratification. Fossil fuel executives are right now planning to burn six times the amount of carbon the atmosphere can tolerate. Ignoring the limits of the planet will precipitate a backlash. We can see it or not—but we cannot avoid it.

We have reached the point where the greatest threat to our security is our desire to consume more. Like the father who by his generosity seduces his son into outsized self-confidence, the fossil fuel industry is deliberating seducing consumers into believing they will escape consequences. Consumers, industry, and the prodigal all share the illusion that they control what they clearly cannot.

The parable portrays how the father's preference for the younger provokes the envy of his elder son. As Esau hated Jacob, so the elder son hates the younger. That same is true, in today's world, of the dispossessed who envy those of us who are not.[4] Like the younger son who is promoted, we

---

4. Genesis does not leave Esau debilitated by envy. This elder brother's transformation of that "dirtiest of emotions" into graciousness is beautifully revealed when, after decades of separation, the two brothers reunite. Jacob, trembling in anticipation of his brother's revenge, instead encounters a mature stranger. Using five of the most attractive

are convinced of our worthiness. Speaking into the vast stretches of the universe, we are inclined to say, "God bless America," not "God bless Iraq or Iran or Nigeria." We fail to see that the dispossessed, were they able, would subdue us. Ever out of reach is the only solution—sharing.

A less obvious aspect of the parable, one informed by the entire prophetic tradition, is that the younger sibling might just possibly emerge from the trauma of his father's generosity. The depiction of the younger son's humiliation is tempered throughout by hints that he might yet achieve self-discipline, that he may become a responsible adult. Likewise, a fragile hope rests on humanity's current indecision as to whether, at this dangerously late hour, we will curb our self-aggrandizing and embrace discipline. Failing that, we will be restricted to doing only that which is allowed by a constricted future.

---

words in the Bible, Esau tells his astonished sibling, "I have enough, my brother" (Gen 33:9).

10

A Samaritan and a Jew
(The Parable of the Good Samaritan)

The Situation

A man was going down from Jerusalem to Jericho,
and fell into the hands of robbers,
who stripped him, beat him,
and went away, leaving him half dead.

Scene I

Now by chance a priest was going down that road;
and when he saw him,
he passed by on the other side.
So likewise a Levite,
when he came to the place and saw him,
passed by on the other side.

Scene II

But a Samaritan while traveling came near him;
and when he saw him, he was moved with pity.
He went to him and bandaged his wounds,
having poured oil and wine on them.
Then he put him on his own animal,
brought him to an inn, and took care of him.

Scene III

The next day he took out two denarii,
gave them to the innkeeper, and said,
"Take care of him; and when I come back,
I will repay you whatever more you spend."

(Luke 10:30–35 NRSV)

INTRODUCTION

The parable about the Samaritan who ministers to a wounded Jew is built around characters who are separated, not by social and economic differences, but by ethnic loyalties. The present chapter explores how this narrative becomes a useful metaphor for probing the strife-filled domains of intolerance that are as prevalent today as they were then. The consequences are enormous. Inside this intolerance may be discovered a fountainhead of climate breakdown denial.

The narrative embraces two related cultures split apart by animosity. While each side worships the same God, both are driven by resentments nurtured across centuries of alienation. The violent origins of their shared prejudice are lost in the dimness of history. The immediate crisis results from a massive accumulation of historic hurt. The downstream consequences of that earlier violence set off intense reactive emotions.

When trying to describe Jewish/Samaritan relations in the early first century, historians are hampered by the dearth of documentary evidence. None exists from the Samaritan side. Most of what survives from the Jewish side, especially from the Jewish historian Josephus, is contaminated by antipathy. The Samaritans traced their ancestry back to Manasseh and Ephraim, two of the ten tribes living in Northern Israel who were exiled by the Assyrians in 721 BCE. About 128 BCE, John Hyrcanus, the Hasmonean high priest in Jerusalem, destroyed the Samaritan temple on Mt. Gerizim. The Samaritans remained loyal to the Gerizim site, and a core of them gathered around nearby Sychar (the reputed site of Jacob's well where the Johannine Jesus meets the Samaritan woman). The Samaritans were "concerned with observing the law of the Torah and most likely had their own particular traditions about that law." Historians can recount five or six events dating from the first century that give evidence of the strong hatred existing between these two peoples.[1]

These cultural siblings, "Jew" and "Samaritan," have long been alienated. Each has a Torah. Each has a temple. For one to belong, the other must not. Forced to live in proximity, they relate by shunning. The Jewish position, represented by the wounded Jew, involves a full-scale rejection of anything Samaritan. "Jews do not share things in common with Samaritans" (John 4:9). Because the parable is addressed only to Jews, it employs "priest" and "Levite" in order to enlarge upon its overall theme of distance. The Samaritans, of course, resolutely mirror the Jewish stance. (An obvious analogy is today's tension between Israelis and Palestinians.)

The parable never announces the intolerant ethos outright. In never even identifies the ethnicity of the man in the ditch. Instead, it carefully leaves the conclusion about who that ambiguous figure might be to story participants and listeners. Listeners are indeed given strong hints that the man is a Jew. First, the narrative names the quintessential Jewish cities of Jerusalem and Jericho (a specificity found nowhere else in the parable corpus). Second is the fact, pointed out by Robert W. Funk, that the Jerusalem/Jericho road, because it went northeast, was used as a detour by northbound Jewish travelers for the explicit purpose of avoiding Samaria.[2] This hinting at ethnicity in order to evoke prejudice is but one example of the parable creator's remarkable indirection. It is up to listeners to make the linkage—and then live with it. By assuming the wounded man is a Jew, most listeners place themselves directly in the path of a coming collision of sensibilities.

---

1. See Isser, "Samaritans and Their Sects," 578.
2. Funk, *Parables and Presence*, 33.

THE JEW

Remarkably, in a context where prejudice leads to control, the parable denies the wounded Jew a voice. He is unconscious and helpless. He remains silent. The overarching ethnic bias he represents is never expressed. Even the fact of his Jewishness is veiled. No word passes between the two protagonists. What the Jew represents is never articulated. Listeners are left on their own to explore the conflict embedded in this story. The narrative powerfully embodies the various ways mutual estrangement blocks contact. It limits contact to one brilliant moment of compassion—occurring in a context of trauma, immobility, and voicelessness. Any larger interaction is stillborn.

Unlike his colleagues, the wounded Jew is in no position to assert his proclivity to shun the Samaritan. No data describe whether or not he accepts the Samaritan's intervention. Nevertheless, while he cannot prevent, overcome, or discourage the Samaritan, he emphatically has not given this despised alien permission to violate the established norms of distance. In fact, he is unprepared to entertain any aspect of the Samaritan's concern. Were he able to speak he would almost certainly have parried this unwelcome compassion.[3] In this magnificently constructed parable, empathy may be extended only to a recipient who is first rendered unconscious—as if he were a patient under anesthesia.

In the realm of prejudice, those who are dominant must create formidable barriers to insulate themselves from the pain they inflict. They must become numb. Thus, they don protective layers of detachment. Institutionalizing their behavior enables them to transform intolerance into rectitude. Although the pain may continue unrelieved, those inflicting it remain securely walled off within their own validating structures.

These long-established protective layers not only dull the ability of dominant players to listen to those they oppress, but they also frustrate any outside effort to empathize with the oppressors' need for control. While the oppressed directly experience the onslaughts of domination, their oppressors have greater ability to conceal any distress or doubt, not only from others but also from themselves. They are certain of their position and powerful enough to prevent others from questioning it. They offer few footholds to anyone trying to scale the sheer cliffs of their confident façade.

---

3. I owe this observation to a 2006 lecture given by Lane C. McGaughy.

Listeners—those who would comprehend how they could so readily impose pain—encounter seamless rationalizations.

THE PRIEST AND THE LEVITE

This story embraces an insistent irony in racist prejudice. "Since you have the power now, your ethnic group dominates mine—and I hate you for it. When I have the power, I will dominate you." Because he is traumatized, the Jew's attitude towards Samaritans is muted, leaving any prejudice to be expressed by intermediaries—a priest and a Levite who can be seen as two versions of one character. Together they quietly enact the defining attitudes trapped within the victim.

Although both the priest and Levite are represented as being inclined to ignore someone in distress, the matter is more complex. These subordinates belong to established groups that are well-defended against any challenge to their way of being. Unlike the symbolic Jew, the priest and Levite do not determine what is expected of them. Instead, they are followers, schooled to function within specified limits. They embrace the intolerance essential to maintaining their insider status. Yet these are thinking, ethical persons. Far from actively creating harm, each is committed to obedience to the law. Each is given to an intensity of purpose and discipline meant to achieve divine desire.

When the priest and Levite sense the presence of an unidentified person in distress, the need for physical closeness comes into conflict with a need for emotional distance. They find themselves poised suddenly on the boundary between knowing and not wanting to know, a place of intense ambivalence. Their very attentiveness prevents them from being attentive. These passersby know there is something there they need not know. A phrase popular in the psychoanalytic literature some years ago tried to capture the quality of this "knowing," terming it "the unthought known."

The fact that they turn aside so abruptly is evidence of their inner conflict. Neither wants to discover who the injured man is. Neither approaches close enough to find out whether the victim is Jew or Samaritan, poor or rich, alive or dead. They resist learning anything about him. They know that if they discover the man to be a Jew, they will have to imagine what he is feeling. They would then have to wrestle with whether or not to do something. By failing to identify the victim, by leaving room to assume he is a Samaritan, they can avoid taking action. In order to avail themselves of this learned strategy, they manufacture real and imagined fears.

Ironically, in order to shun the stranger, these ethically attuned individuals ignore a fellow Jew in desperate need. Their avoidance is so sweeping that they remain unaware of dilemmas urgently beckoning them from within their own religious tradition. Were the wounded Jew able to cry out, were he to use familiar language and accent, both might have found it considerably more difficult to pass by. How differently the parable would read if the Jew had had the capacity to speak! Had the priest or Levite possessed fuller knowledge, then their refusal to intervene would represent a very different kind of "passing by." The metaphor is brilliant. The listener comes to realize that these subordinates have in fact succeeded in remaining unaware of the toll their commitment to intolerance has taken on their integrity. Preoccupation with what is more important has prevented discovery of what is more urgent. The specter of fear impedes attentiveness to hurt. Loyalty to prejudice excludes allegiance to fellow-feeling.

The parable illustrates how intolerance toward others can be self-destructive. Through their preemptive avoidance, the priest and Levite visit greater harm on a fellow Jew than if they had intended malevolence. That avoidance, in turn, comes from the prejudice inherited from fellow Jews. This instance of "passing by" becomes a potent representation of the ways in which one's need not to know can, with seeming innocence, lead to immense amounts of hurt—not only for people at great distance but for those close at hand.

It should be obvious by now that we are all priests and Levites. It should also be evident how our own ambivalence when confronting modern-day climate breakdown aligns with theirs. Climate breakdown will claim many victims, some with injuries similar to those of the man in the ditch. The priest and Levite become superb examples of the semi-willful not-knowing characteristic of the majority of persons committed to denying climate change. We do not want to look; we refuse to understand that which most infringes our well-being. We live as if the beast is caged, or even nonexistent. We do not acknowledge that it is charging towards us at full tilt. The oligarchs, as usual, celebrate our apathy.

Jesus' Parables Speak to Power and Greed
THE SAMARITAN

The Samaritan is an outsider. He is not in his own country. He lacks the protection found in familiar surroundings. He must endure cultural slurs. He first notices the body from a distance. It is immobile. There is no communication. Like the priest and the Levite, he does not recognize the identity of the figure in the ditch. But, while the latter withdraw into not knowing, the former moves towards discovery. Each step in his "coming nearer" contrasts with each step in their "passing by." At every stage—as he looks, approaches, recognizes, moves forward, feels pity, kneels, and reaches out—the Samaritan must transgress cultural barriers. The discovery that the victim is a Jew does not deter him. He pushes past the "normal" reaction: never, *never* do Jew and Samaritan touch. Undaunted, he binds the wounds of this alien, touching him at length and intimately.

With this remarkable initiative, the Samaritan momentarily transforms the pervasive intolerance surrounding this story. But there the matter stands. When he tries to make contact, when he reaches out, he encounters someone who is unconscious. Since the Jew has not given permission, the initiative of the Samaritan seems unlikely to have any impact on the ongoing prejudice. This shutting down of discourse impedes any potential to demonstrate the respect necessary to form a relationship. After the story is over, how does one go forward?

That question is left to the story's listeners. What kind of bond develops between you and the stranger who has saved your life, even if you hate him? Although you may refuse to speak to him, will you not wonder about him, about how it was that he took the risk when he might not have? The thing will not go away. "I would not be alive today without him." The beliefs, customs, and prejudices that so energize your life all become muddled under the weight of "You saved my life!" This feeling, this emotional reality, means that prior distinctions can no longer function in the way they used to.

We are drawn to ponder the remarkable initiative of the parable's third character. By reaching out to a despised enemy, he enters into shocking conflict with established norms. He momentarily overturns the resentment born of centuries of dispossession. By repudiating the massive historic hurt that might otherwise exacerbate the immediate crisis, the Samaritan thrusts that larger crisis aside. His response is informed by a hard-won ability to empathize. In parallel fashion, our own awareness of what he has achieved, and of the powerful resistance which he has had to overcome, can be acquired only through similarly disciplined empathy.

Robert W. Funk was a pioneer in exploring the ways in which the original Jewish listeners would have struggled to process the Samaritan's intervention. Nearly everyone—priest or Levite, Jew or Samaritan—would have recoiled from the Samaritan's readiness to break through these heavily guarded boundaries.[4] We can follow Funk even further into wondering: How will the wounded Jew himself react when, during his recovery, he learns the identity of the stranger who has saved his life? However he experiences that shocking moment, he certainly will never forget it.

Since the Samaritan does not stand to gain in any obvious way, what could have motivated him? It would appear he is moved to action by his capacity to feel the experience of the other. He feels the pain and helplessness of the Jew. For that to happen, he must overcome the strictures that so separate these two, and that would require years of preparation. It is difficult to exaggerate the amount of work involved. Clearly, he knows what it is like to be defenseless. He will have spent a lifetime struggling against the temptation to withdraw into resentment.

The Samaritan bursts through the barrier of ethnic prejudice, but he in no way dismantles it. The parable leaves to its listeners the work of exploring the impact of the Samaritan's empathy. Such empathy can sometimes threaten an entire way of being. The cost to an oppressor of becoming aware of those oppressed can be high, resulting at least in retaliation from superiors, disdain from peers, and loss of a cherished sense of belonging. The parable now confronts its listeners with a huge amount of work.

THE PARABLE-LISTENER

The parable establishes the fact of cultural norms by providing examples of the behaviors of people caught up in such norms. That conformity can then be used to measure who is "good" and who is "bad." Within the parable itself, an important distinction needs to be made between the dominant person who creates the definitions, and the subordinates who conform to them. The responses of the subordinates are shaped by the attitudes of their superiors. The distinctions between "bad" and "good" are simplistic categories inadequate to describe what is going on.

---

4. See Funk, *Parables and Presence*, 33.

Jesus' Parables Speak to Power and Greed

Modern interpretations, inherited from Luke, most often find the priest and Levite "bad." If we move back to wondering about the pregospel Jewish perceptions (which likely come closer to the perspectives of Jesus' original audiences), this matter of "bad" or "good" becomes less clear. Priest and Levite are seen as "good" to the extent that they represent established piety. They are seen as "bad" from the standpoint of anti-clerical sentiment among the peasants. They are also "bad" to the extent they are caught up in the accepted overall prejudice. However, because that prejudice is as rife among parable-listeners as elsewhere, this final awareness may be a case of the pot calling the kettle black. Put differently, the early listeners most likely to grasp the complex nature of priest/Levite avoidance would be those who were themselves questioning their own conformity to established norms.

Here we arrive at a collision between empathy and prejudice. Because seeing might lead to feeling, those who may possess the potential to feel avoid seeing. Having feelings may result in ambivalence, which in turn might tempt us into difficult and costly action. What lurks is the question: Are the cultural norms in and of themselves just or unjust? That is, do they hurt innocent people? The same structural barriers that protect the characters in the parable from experiencing the consequences of their choices are still alive today, vigorously trying to pass off our willingness to disadvantage others as acceptable.

If you are able to feel the experience of others, you will find yourself engaging their deprivation and hurt. You may also come to realize that your participation in walled-off conformity has left you blind to the ways you are humiliating strangers and failing others nearby who are wounded and dying. Perhaps the best modern analogy here is American racism.

What happens when cultural norms constrict our ability to see and, thereby, limit the ways we choose to act? We learn to believe that it is better not to feel, that our own belonging will be threatened should we dare to engage the experience of another. Here we stumble upon the ways in which elitist needs for insulation have so influenced us. Rather than struggle with where to locate ourselves in the midst of ongoing prejudice, we have reduced our own readings of this parable to a simple example story.

How did we arrive at a place of not being conflicted about participating in hurtful behavior? How do we move from being certain we are not intolerant to becoming aware that we might be oblivious? To lay bare these troublesome questions, the parable features someone who breaks through the established order, punctuates the standard way of doing things, and recovers another way of being. In so doing, it invites listeners to wonder where to place themselves.

Because the Samaritan has resisted retreating into hatred, he leads us, as Virgil leads Dante, into the hell experienced by those whom the oppressors have hurt. By creating openings for us to exercise our own empathy, this story affords us a proving ground to deepen our own awareness not only of what this hero has accomplished but also of what we might possibly do. By animating our ability to empathize, it invokes the single power capable of penetrating the indifference and avoidance so prevalent then and now.

11

Using These Parables to Explore Climate Denial

The dominant figures portrayed in each of the nine parables studied in this book live in isolation from those they control. They can only function by remaining unaware of the persons they are harming. They take whatever they want without reference to the feelings of those they deprive. They refuse to hear the protests coming from below. Those who dominate must persuade themselves that their methods of control, whether blatant or disguised, are warranted, despite the damage they inflict. In these stories, it is inevitably the superior, never the subordinate, who is aggrieved. The narratives of those who dominate perpetually erase the narratives of those who are dominated. Each parable hints at the enormous amount of work needed to bridge the gap separating the victim from his dominators. And the superior—by putting himself forward as all-knowing and by silencing protests—introduces serious complications. Because of these complications, in the context of modern climate change denial, the parables become exceedingly important stories for our time.

Unless informed by listener empathy, every parable remains a tragedy. One of the largest impediments to engaging in their empathetic work is the perception that the superior character represents God, that is, someone whose powerful judgment or mercy intervenes to make things right. These interpretations thus render unnecessary, and thereby useless, the already muted and distorted protests from below. They deny the listener an appreciation of a whole range of possibilities, in particular the experience of those dominated.

By turning attention to the effects of domination, the parables invite listeners to reflect on the ways aristocracies across centuries have justified their control over the resources of the many. Listeners can be drawn to ponder how they themselves might respond to someone usurping their rights. This, in turn, can lead to the discovery that "the kingdom of God" may not be a place away from here and in the future, but rather a state of mind and heart to be discovered in the here and now; not a destination to be inhabited but rather a beckoning to be realized; not a situation of comfort but rather an invitation to empathy.

HOW DIFFERENCES IN CONTROL IN THE PARABLES ANTICIPATE DIFFERENCES IN CLIMATE DENIAL

Jesus locates each of these stories precisely at the tenuous intersection between the powerful and the vulnerable. As no one sees into those doing the damage better than those to whom the damage is done, enlarging upon the response of the subordinate can open up an avenue to better understanding the superior. But, if we are to look to the subordinates to find a way forward, we must first overcome the temptation to look down on them. It is uphill work.

In order to ensure that they themselves never endure humiliation, parable superiors have long circumvented any curiosity about what their underlings might be trying to tell them. Instead, they expect listeners to join them in denigrating their subordinates and rendering them voiceless. Like modern plutocrats, they override and silence any protest from below. They distract listeners from observing what is truly going on by attributing malevolent behaviors to their subordinates. In the absence of an alternative narrative, listeners can be readily persuaded by the authoritative conviction of the dominant character that his subordinates are at fault.

Perhaps the most significant moment in each parable occurs when the still-surviving, albeit distorted, protest of the underling confronts the out-of-control demand of the overlord to possess "more"—control, money, rectitude. While the potential for finding common ground varies widely, it is only just possible. It is at this moment that these stories become remarkable commentaries on the vicissitudes of climate change denial.

Jesus' Parables Speak to Power and Greed

The superior characters in these narratives represent a range of intention, starting with those who are so focused on their purposes that they are indifferent to any and all costs to others. In their absolute commitment to using their power to gratify their selfish desires, the judge and talentmaster stand head and shoulders over the others. They harm others intentionally and with calculation. Their sadism differs only in its motivation. What for the judge is a matter of emotional need is for the talentmaster a matter of profit. Both are so engrossed in their goals as to be unreachable.

The risky insistence of the widow and the disguised cowering of the third slave lay bare the single-minded purpose of their superiors. As the judge is the least likely to acknowledge his involvement in the parable's tragedy, it is no wonder the predominant response to his intractability is to call upon God to intervene. There exists more room for listener intervention when the talentmaster rides roughshod over the effort by the slave to open his master's eyes to the harm he is doing. Though the slave must maintain a precarious balance between opposing his master's greed while not insisting his master admit to that greed, he has at least begun to speak. Listeners have a fighting chance to see what is going on.

The other stories also expose large fissures in relationships, but they afford listeners greater opportunities to bridge those gaps. In the parable of the tenants and the landowner, for instance, the landowner is still attracted to the sanctioning force of law. Because he proceeds calmly with lawful precision, he gives listeners a pretext for appealing to comprehensive law. However, when he misinterprets his tenants' inarticulate message—delivered in the form of wounded slaves—things become more complex, less certain, and more open to possibility. At that point listeners have a better chance of glimpsing the superior's responsibility for his subordinates' rebellion. Because he refuses to recognize that he is insulting them, the landowner provokes his tenant farmers' rage—and listeners find themselves having to comprehend murder.

Like lower-class victims today, the parable subordinates are insufficiently aware of the true sources of their distress. Each is vulnerable to the influence of the superior's judgment. The underlings remain defeated while the overlord emerges unscathed. (Such escapist blaming is the way of imperialists the world over.) They are unable to modify their superiors' violence. Instead, they assimilate and reenact that violence.

Next, in the parable of the unforgiving slave, we encounter the efforts of the slavemaster to release his slave from indebtedness. Here we find an attempt, however compromised, to craft a creative resolution to impasse. This master hopes to induce change in his subordinate, but the slave appears to rebuff his master. He thus exposes a serious miscalculation in his master's effort at releasing him from his debt. The slave's action is informed not by his master's newfound magnanimity but rather by his lifelong—and still ongoing—pattern of behavior. He would release his slave from his control without for a moment relinquishing his grip. As he is unable to comprehend his slave's mimicry of his own coercive behavior, the master lashes out. Listeners are invited to see both the irony and the tragedy in this sequence.

The subordinates have taken on board their superiors' belief in the efficacy of coercion. They do to their fellows what their superiors have done to them. The "unforgiving" slave chokes his fellow. The tenants injure their master's slaves. (Here is a beginning articulation of the modern plutocrats' strategy of displacing their victims' hostility towards themselves onto those even less fortunate.) On some occasions, subordinates even turn the coercion on themselves. When the rich man neglects his manager, for example, the manager eviscerates his own competencies. The younger son is overwhelmed by self-inflicted shame. Such destructive behavior secretly pleases the superior, who thereby escapes responsibility for the inadequacies he has himself provoked. In order to "forgive" the deficiencies for which he is responsible, he has only to ignore the pernicious consequence of his own need to be needed.

In these parables, the dominant figures are completely oblivious to the ways in which their refusal to acknowledge having done harm does more harm than the original harm itself. Take, for instance, the most famous story of all—the prodigal son. Listeners to this day are distracted by the story's focus on "forgiveness." But that which the father forgives is in fact an aberration of his own making. The father agreed, astonishingly, that the son is entitled to consume his father's resources. He rejoices in his act of generosity, but his son burns with shame. When the prodigal returns home, he is not *at* home—he won't be until and unless his father can acknowledge the control hidden in his seeming generosity. In parallel fashion, the rich man cannot see the connection between his neglect of his trusted manager and that manager's collapse. By dismissing his manager's efforts to act out that neglect, he undermines the man's ability to avoid his impending destruction.

Jesus' Parables Speak to Power and Greed

Here we encounter ever-increasing ambiguity about the intentions of the superiors. For the slavemaster to release his unforgiving slave would require him to loosen his grip; although he tries, he cannot. For the landlord to avoid exposing his son to mortal peril this would require him to acknowledge the perfidy of his ancestors; he cannot even begin to imagine that. The loving father would be appalled at his destructiveness. The vineyard owner is so preoccupied with establishing his own righteousness that he cannot grasp the degree to which he shames his workers. None of these actors desires the outcomes they produce. Their failure to see, although catastrophic, is not deliberate. Their loss is unanticipated. The householder has no intention to do harm. He struggles to decide how to respond to the poor he has inadvertently invited into his world. He simply does not know whether he will take them in or eject them. Similarly, knowing and not knowing at the same time, the priest and Levite pass by a suffering that touches only on the very edge of their awareness.

One way through this morass, one way the parables broaden the possibility for understanding the experience of subordinates, can be found in how these stories condense lengthy sequences into seeming brief spans of time. These sequences comprise increasingly broken connections that have, over time, come to be accepted as normal. The insidious conversion of custom into "law" gradually makes room for the overlord's self-justifying certainties. By the end of this sequence the superior has convinced both himself and others of his right to dominate. In this narrative realm, it is listeners who must enter the no-man's land between the world of the superior and the world of the subordinate. Listeners are called upon to explore the breakdown between these two worlds and to restore their connection. They can settle for blaming the victim, or they can become aware of, and struggle with, the lengthy histories over the course of which the dominant character became an abuser.

This entire chapter emphasizes the expectation that, rather than acceding to the overlord's judgments, listeners will exercise their own independent judgment and recognize the ways in which they have assented to the perspective of the superior character.

HOW THE PARABLES AWAKEN RESISTANCE

Throughout human history, two worlds have coexisted—rich and poor, free and enslaved, those who dominate and those who are dominated. The dominant wealthy believe they can control everyone else. Climate denial represents just one aspect of this conviction. In depicting the fearsome resistance confronting those who would challenge the hegemony of the powerful, Jesus' parables pull no punches. Subordinates are left with no choice but to endure what they cannot prevent. Just as Jesus' early hearers are cowed by the definitions of the powerful, so modern listeners bow to distortions imposed from above. However, while such narratives, both then and now, portray a superior who appears to offer generosity and lawfulness, they can also be seen as describing the reality that, for these same protagonists, the law is abolished, distance grows, guilt is erased, and self-deception increases.

Each parable demonstrates the lack of empathy and understanding for the oppressed by the oppressors. The same is true of the stories imposed by powerful climate deniers, for their power depends on ignorance of the long history of encroachment on human limits and, more recently, on planetary limits. Though centuries of trespass have resulted in the out-of-control emission of carbon dioxide into a packed atmosphere and saturated oceans, this overreach is accepted as the "normal" or "inevitable" consequence of economic growth. Few persons are shocked—or terrified.

When learning how to confront climate change denial, we need stories that portray the disguised malevolence of ingrained privilege, narratives that call upon us to hear the muted voices of the underlings. Jesus invites us to enter into their experience and to join him at the bottom of the pile. We must step back from the church's later elevation of Jesus as LORD and return him to his place in history, as one of the poor. For Western middle-class observers who have rarely known subjugation, rarely been hungry, and rarely been deprived of their voice, such an empathic task is formidable.

In a remarkable passage, Marguerite Yourcenar captures in subtle tones the weighty presence of silence fashioned, over centuries, in the service of hierarchy. In memoirs addressed to his seventeen-year-old son, she has the Roman Emperor Hadrian remark,

> Rank, position, all such hazards tend to restrict the field of vision for the student of mankind: my slave has totally different facilities for observing me from what I possess for observing him, but his means to do so are as limited as my own. Every morning for twenty years, old Euphorion has handed me my flask of oil and my sponge, but my knowledge of him ends with his acts of service, and his knowledge of me ends with my bath; any effort of the part

Jesus' Parables Speak to Power and Greed

of either emperor or slave to learn more straightway produces the effect of an indiscretion.[1]

What Yourcenar so sensitively intimates can be summarized in staccato terms. The listener begins to imagine how an underling actually feels when forced into submission, enticed into mimicry, subverted into self-blame, and ignored. By entering from below, listeners can feel the weight of being dominated, of being told how to be, of being rewarded for complying and punished for resisting, of being forbidden to be oneself. How they should accept the definitions imposed on them by the superior. How they have to devote so much of their energy to dissembling, holding in, or disguising their speech, and how they are at fault if they do not. Alert observers discover how thoroughly underlings are blamed and ostracized for reintroducing descriptions that have been suppressed by the self-serving definitions of the powerful.

Jesus invites his listeners to join in the experience of those looking up from below, but nowhere does he encourage it. Just as the superior character in the parable offers no help in this task, neither, astonishingly, does the author of these stories. The realities of the existence of the subordinates have been loaded into the narratives without a single word devoted to their description. Jesus carefully, thoughtfully, deliberately assigns the work of discovery to his listeners. In order to grasp the experience of the underling, we must first free ourselves of the culturally sanctioned deceptions so deftly embedded in these narratives. Just as we must see through the disguises employed by those who dominate to hide their true purposes, so we must work to revise the distorted and silenced experience of those who are dominated.

Who will enter this no-man's land between powerful entitlement and helpless frustration? How much of what is claimed as ignorance is merely our refusal to see, because if we see we will know exactly what needs doing? Like the priest and Levite, we sense that someone over there in the ditch may be *in* trouble and, therefore, may *be* trouble. It is at that exact moment we turn away. We have seen enough to stop seeing. We must then attempt to become unaware of our decision not to be aware.

Will we be complicit in allowing these parable worlds to be compartmentalized into those who blame and those who are blamed? Will we leave both the superior and the subordinate engulfed in tragedy? Will the one who dominates continue to command the power to define? Can the abused

1. Yourcenar, *Memoirs of Hadrian*, 22–23.

subordinate break free from these controlling definitions? Or is it up to the listener to modify the conditions of interaction? In the present reading, Jesus entrusts to his listeners the work of bringing these two worlds together. Then and now, these stories function as an exceptional proving ground for grappling with widely promoted and helplessly tolerated inequality.

Both the superior and the subordinate are preoccupied with either maintaining power or escaping degradation. Neither is likely to tackle the task of understanding the other. Those most likely to engage will come neither from above or below but rather from somewhere in between. Jesus may originally have addressed his parables primarily to the retainer classes, those inhabiting the world between the aristocracy and the peasantry—soldiers, bankers, scribes, tax gatherers, and others. Often charged with facilitating the accumulation of wealth, some of these retainers might question their role in exploiting this divide. The third slave in the parable of the talents is the primary example of such a figure.

In today's world, this group would include those who are neither devoted to acquiring "more" nor preoccupied with losing what little they have. They are sufficiently well-off to have avoided being co-opted. Their economic advantage positions them both to accept the necessary sacrifices of engagement and to reject the short-term benefits of denial. They are, thus, better able to entertain the imperatives encountered in global warming.

By understanding both sides, neither trusting the overlord nor reproaching the underling, not hoping for rescue or escaping into blame, we grasp how each narrative describes an inexorable movement towards inevitable tragedy. What does God wish for in this situation, we wonder. Do we want to embody that divine desire? We must take our cues from the subordinate figures—the widow, the third slave, the Samaritan. They occupy a position similar to that of the listener. They can see, but only if they first look; they can understand, but only after they first feel.

The work of overcoming climate denial is analogous to entering into the experience of parable subordinates. If the heat were upon us, if we had no clean water, if climate refugees were pounding on our doors, we would not need to do the creative work required to hear them. Like the shadows of figures boxing, the parables weave and dodge. To appreciate the as-yet-out-of-reach feelings of parable subordinates, listeners must move from shadow to body, from suggestion to substance. This demand holds true not just for action and movement, but even more so for feeling and emotion. Listeners must call to mind hatred so strong it can lead to murder, jealousy so powerful it can drive a lifelong wedge between brothers, prejudice so intense that one human can pass by the suffering of another. They must understand that centuries of structural oppression can leave victims with a smoldering anger so hot that even well-meaning charity can cause it to burst into flame.

With the talentmaster and the judge, listeners find themselves feeling the anger incited by those in power. No one holds the dominant persons responsible for what they do. No one challenges their unrelieved injustices with the incisive authority of an ancient prophet, such as Nathan, who, in confronting the betrayer King David, declares to his face, "*You* are the man!" (2 Sam 12:7). The closest any of the parables in this corpus comes to direct confrontation is found in the surreptitious moment when the third slave buries his entrusted talent of silver. Only he dares articulate the pain these lords impose on their people. Elsewhere in these stories, the pall of ancient slavery and the impoverishment of smallholder peasants is swallowed up in the self-assured entitlement of the powerful.

Because there was no middle class to provide a buffer, in Jesus' time the maldistribution of wealth was even more destructive than it is now. Still, in spite of the progress made since the Industrial Revolution, the unequal distribution of wealth remains high. In the United States, excessive wealth is likely *the* major force undermining democratic institutions. The very rich mobilize the frustrations of the white working class by deflecting anger, that should rightly be aimed at themselves, towards more immediately vulnerable people of color and immigrants. Jesus' parables similarly seem to invite the listener to deflect the anger that should be directed at the wealthy onto subordinates. These subordinates, in turn, appear to deserve that censure.

However, Jesus subtly lures his listeners to question that assumption. His attack on wealth is not an attack on the wealthy. Rather he probes the distortions imposed by wealth, in particular the trap of forever wanting "more" that wealth springs on its possessors, and which, in turn, exacerbates the need for even more sophisticated rationales for their rapacious behavior.

When our grandchildren and their children look back on the 1970s, 80s, 90s, and 2000s, they will surely ask, "How much more could you have done to prevent our current suffering—but did not do?" Our response is to observe that we were bedeviled by narratives imposed across five millennia. Stories justifying the dominance of the few over the many have been with us since the beginnings of settled agriculture. We were fighting entrenched interests and venerable credentials. The various aristocracies who pursue "more" have always been successful at ignoring anything that threatens their interests. The poor have never had the leverage to oppose those deeply entrenched stories. The few challengers of note—Karl Marx, for instance—were portrayed as devils incarnate. Then one circumstance—namely, the abrupt arousal of the laws of physics—changed, and it was earth-shattering.

For thousands of years the curves representing global temperatures were monotonously flat. Only in the late twentieth century did they suddenly make a sharp turn upwards. The unexpected trigger was the appearance of a nonhuman opponent. Narratives sufficient to explain this shift could not keep pace. No story has yet been able to capture the massive significance of this unstoppable gut punch.

Like religious people, we try to counter ambiguity by creating narratives of certainty. So, too, do fossil fuel executives. Throughout the ages, denial has been an essential element of narratives justifying the domination of the many by the few. Rex Tillerson's offhand comment, "We'll adapt," is an example. The power of these stories derives from the ability of their authors to have them appear true. Only now has the prospect of nature's retaliation loomed so large as to undermine these fictions—but not yet large enough to overcome them. The parables of Jesus had the potential to keep pace, but they were transformed into accounts of God intervening to rescue us from our choices. Thus, we lost a major opportunity to recover narratives that might have helped us cope.

What played out then between two individuals plays out now between powerful oligarchs and most of humanity. Only the scale differs. Modern fossil fuel executives have access to the same two options: dedicated concern for the well-being of millions or focused concern with the making of millions. Lacking empathy to guide their decision-making and relying only on self-interest, these executives fail to notice that their choices are, in fact, undermining their own interests.

How can they not see what is going to happen? One would think that they might at least keep a sharp eye out for how political and social reactions to climate change are likely to affect their bottom line. The answer is that they do, but they only see the immediate bottom line. While the social and economic realities affecting future profits are not difficult to discern, and although executives have been well schooled by their scientists, they insist on pursuing plans to put far more carbon into the atmosphere than humanity can tolerate, as if future generations will not exist.

Here we encounter an egregious abdication of responsibility, made more reprehensible because it is undertaken in full awareness of the repercussions. All the reasons for climate change denial by the powerful can be reduced to one dimension: immediate profit. While choosing not to know about the future might interfere with long-term profits, the alternative—knowing about the future—would almost certainly interfere with short-term profits. When conflict crops up between near-term profits for the corporation and long-term obligations to the wider population, one's responsibility is to the goals of the organization, not the needs of the public. Corporate loyalty brooks no challenge to the systemic injustices that are part and parcel of profit-taking.

Of course, we cannot know the internal thinking of these leaders. But, even if they were privately clear about the stark contrasts outlined above, they would never acknowledge any ambivalence in public. The intense competition among fossil fuel corporations prevents any single company from taking the first step. Regardless of how much is obvious or hidden from them, they will conceal what they know from outsiders. Their power completely protects their privacy. Like the rich man, they will exit their responsibilities by persuading the public that they have done well.

The lifetime commitment to corporate loyalties systematically excises any empathy for victims. It facilitates the easy dismissal of concerns both for the environment and for the long-term interests of stockholders. Such cultivated lack of empathy allows denial to thrive. Of course, some corporations are responsible to the public and to the environment, but the fossil fuel industry does not number among them. Its leaders are cornered. They cannot reconcile concern for public well-being with profits for shareholders.

The shift from candor to deception whenever corporate profits are threatened is both commonplace and experienced as necessary. If a cost-effective alternative exists within which they can still honor their social contract, they will do so. But if it is clear they cannot square the two, they will choose profit-making. They will minimize or ignore any future realities that endanger current profits. The justifications used to silence any who protest are many. For example, "If we don't do it our competitors will," and "Our hands are tied; our shareholders will not tolerate the loss in profits."

Given the invincibility of the opponent the fossil fuel industry is attempting to overcome, this commonplace shift becomes immensely

Using These Parables to Explore Climate Denial

important. Put simply, you can crowd climate change out of awareness, but you cannot defeat it. It is here for the long haul. Your efforts at denial serve only to make it more dangerous. In response, the executive declares simply, "I will not, on my watch, acknowledge these concerns," thus ignoring an unpalatable truth and embracing a time-limited illusion.

In eight of the nine extant narrative parables (the exception being the good Samaritan) the superior exploits the inferior. The parables thus foreshadow Naomi Klein's insight, which she calls "the Shock Doctrine."[2] The oligarchs introduce distortions in the distribution of wealth or power, thereby revealing their lack of concern for the well-being of those they are depriving. When the superior steals the wealth or well-being of the subordinate, the subordinate rebels in ways readily identified as inappropriate or "bad." Because they cannot fight their overlords, they either turn on each other or on themselves. The oligarchs use this chaos to justify the imposition of further political and economic controls.

This pattern will be incorporated into the various sequences of climate breakdown. Listeners must decide whether to join the oppressive overlords or the fragmented underlings, that is, whether to accept or reject the oligarchs' efforts to transfer responsibility. They cannot not decide. At stake is listener support for various oppressed groups to unite rather than be splintered by the prior corruption of the oligarchs.

The listener has the advantage of possessing some degree of empathy. That the wealthy do not is a direct consequence of their possession of power. It is precisely the lack of empathy, of this means of understanding reality, that makes their possession of power so dangerous. It prevents them from seeing the downside of the remarkable "success" they celebrate, namely, the deprivation of the vast array of underprivileged. Their inability to imagine the experience of the oppressed forever blocks their ability to understand that, as the future unfolds, the desperation resulting from the cascading disturbances of climate change will mobilize previously passive segments of the poor. When that happens, it will not suffice merely to allow massive numbers of deaths. The powerful will be forced to actively engineer them.

Access to space for the absorption of CO_2 waste is a crucial economic asset. Limits on access will necessarily curtail economic development. At the United Nations conference on climate change (UN COP)[3], an attempt

---

2. Klein, *This Changes Everything*.

3. COP is the informal name for the annual Conference of the Parties to the United Nations Framework Convention on Climate Change (UNFCCC). The UNFCCC was

is underway to apportion responsibility, to both rich and poor nations, for the shortage of future space in the atmospheric commons. Because the resource is finite, exploitation of that space by some will necessarily limit similar exploitation by others. It will require that some be dispossessed. The one force that might prevent this outcome, namely, feeling what it is like to be dispossessed, is easily disregarded. The irony is that awareness of the other may be the only thing capable of saving us.

Our inability to acknowledge the fact of limited atmospheric space fits with the dominant narrative of unending economic growth—to have less is to lose, to have more is to gain. We reject the scientific evidence because it challenges this narrative of economic expansion. We not only refuse to accept the bankruptcy of the narrative, we also ignore the fact that it is destroying us. But no one wants to miss out on the gains that can still be realized in service to our institutions. No one will risk stepping forward.

People accustomed to post-World War II economic success are now facing deprivations brought on by climate change. In the decades in between those two events, plutocrats sucked up the earth's resources. The foundations of their prosperity—which is already threatened by the maldistribution of wealth—are slowly being eaten away by invisible particles of carbon. Their familiar world of malleable human boundaries has given way to one of unyielding, nonhuman limits. In response, plutocrats resort to far-fetched denial. They believe they can overcome nonnegotiable limits, using strategies ranging from magical video games to magical scientific adaptations. It is as if the sea-ice melting away from our coastlines will rise up from the oceans to reform as glaciers.

---

adopted in 1992 at the Rio Earth Summit, which marked the beginning of the international community's first concerted effort to confront the problem of climate change.

12

Empathy

You can address anything as a "thou" and you can feel the change in your psychology as you do it . . . The ego that sees a "thou" is not the same ego as sees an "it."

Your whole psychology changes when you address things as an "it."

—Joseph Campbell[1]

INTRODUCTION

Mark's commentary on Jesus' parables contains a puzzling statement.

> And he said to them, "everything comes in parables; in order that (*hina*) 'they may indeed look, but not perceive, and may indeed listen but not understand.'"
>
> (Mark 4:11–12 NRSV paraphrasing Isa 6:9; see also Luke 8:11)

The Greek conjunction *hina* used by Mark in paraphrasing Isaiah can be understood to mean either "in order that" or "so that." The parallel saying in Luke reads, "I speak in parables '*so that* looking they may not perceive, and listening they may not understand'" (11:8:10–11 NRSV). It is unclear how

1. Campbell, *Power of Myth*, 99.

best to translate *hina* in Mark's verse. Even more perplexing is what Mark is trying to communicate through it.

Whatever Mark's intention in referencing the prophet Isaiah, if we understand this to mean that we are precluded from grasping the power of the parables, then this saying stands in clear tension with a fundamental saying of Jesus, found in various forms in both the Sayings Gospel Q and the Gospel of Thomas: "So I say to you, 'Ask, and it will be given you; search, and you will find; knock, and the door will be opened for you'" (Luke 11:9; see also Matt 7:7). "Jesus said, 'Those who seek should not stop seeking until they find'" (Thom 2:1; see also Thom 92:1, 94:1–2.)

The seeming conflict between Mark's use of *hina* and these incontrovertible sayings of the historical Jesus seems to suggest that although what the parables offer is not readily accessible, it is open to determined inquiry. In these stories, Jesus stops far short of revealing or proposing an easy insight. His teaching requires the listener's hard-won participation in the form of sustained attention, difficult work, inquiry, wondering, perseverance, and, above all, the exercise of empathy. The question is not what is being given but how it is received.

The intent of the parables is not to obscure reality but to represent it. As with any great works of art, they offer a wealth of understanding. They do not indulge listeners. They do not confront them. Rather, these narratives oblige listeners to do the work necessary to discover what is truly going on. This involves penetrating layers of deception and betrayal. It means rejecting the temptation to idealize the superior and, by default, letting him do the work of resolving the narrative's difficulties. It involves getting past the inclination to blame the subordinate for what is, clearly, reprehensible behavior. It requires comprehending the larger social and economic structures that contain and control both parties—ancient imperialism, slavery, extortion, land-grabbing, all paralleled by today's imperialism, militarism, unrestrained financial manipulation, racism, poverty, and now, ecological disaster. We take hold of these parables in a manner similar to the way we grasp the shape of our troubled world.

THE WAY THROUGH: FEELING WHAT IT IS LIKE TO BE THE OTHER PERSON

We cannot counter the self-centered greed which lies at the heart of the destructiveness of climate change by appealing to the top echelons of our society. We cannot get through by appealing to science. Nor will we succeed by appealing to God's intervention. The only way through may be that of the Samaritan or the third talent slave, that is, finding a way into the experience of the other and recognizing that experience within ourselves. Asking how we would feel if we were in their shoes. The parables show characters lacking empathy, but require empathy to understand them. Ironically, the Samaritan's effort to empathize succeeds only because the figure in the ditch is unconscious. It is improbable that the wounded man would welcome the Samaritan's ministrations. He is more likely to pull back from contact or even rail at his rescuer. But, by crossing over, the Samaritan makes a critical beginning. Likewise, the third slave makes a beginning by refusing to be complicit. And by standing up to the judge, so does the widow.

All of these figures illustrate how Jesus confronts power. In the face of enormous resistance, he does not appeal to his God to intervene. Nor does he lay out conditions for his listeners to follow. Instead, he invites us—in kinship with the widow, the third slave, and the Samaritan—to exercise empathy. As with them, our awakened feelings for the underling will not overcome the dominance of the overlords, but it will transform our own experience.

EMPATHY

To "empathize" does not mean to "sympathize." To be empathic means to experience how another person feels and thinks. This reaching out to comprehend the perspective of another does not mean we have to agree with it. Empathy lets us apprehend negative as well as positive experiences. It involves working to get past mere reactivity. It entails making an effort to comprehend how the behavior of someone else—however puzzling or insufferable—represents, from that person's point of view, the best option available. It demands sustained attention. It requires careful observation of one's own feelings. For example, if I should find myself feeling inexplicably angry in someone's presence, there's a good chance that that person, in spite of appearances, is also angry. Such understanding is central to any relationship; it becomes the compass for navigating the emotional world.

In the face of climate change denial, our ability to empathize may be the one dimension of human experience most able to save us from self-destruction. As Charles Dickens conveyed so well in his depiction of Scrooge, the only force able to put the brakes on our greed is our ability to sense how we make other people feel. Unfortunately for our civilization, that impulse is not likely to come about of our own initiative. It is more likely to be forced on us by the chance collision of a massive climate-induced disaster with the immediate well-being of affluent sectors of society. If it does not come too late, it would be a fortuitous collision.

Standing side by side with our wish for a rescuing God is our aversion to doing the difficult work of empathizing. When we divide parable characters into categories of "all-good" and worthy of respect, and "all-bad" and deserving of punishment, we miss the tension that permeates the parable. Each character misunderstands the other. Only the listener is able to see both sides, but developing that capacity is far from easy. The most distasteful thing about engaging representatives of climate denial is having to understand (but not agree with) attitudes and actions we do not respect.

We sometimes avoid embracing empathy because we expect to be bored. "Why should I choose to spend five years of my life, like the sociologist Hochschild, living among people with whom I disagree and who I expect will have little of interest to offer?" The answer is that sustained empathy, involving respect and the winning of trust, can lead to unexpected engagements. "I didn't think you cared. I didn't think I could trust you. That's why I didn't tell you."

We also avoid empathy because it can be dangerous, especially for those caught up in corporate loyalty. Speaking out on behalf of persons being harmed by corporate decisions threatens those in control. In this context, empathy is seen as weakness. It can lead to accusations that the whistleblower is unfit. Stereotyping, blaming, and demeaning of difference helps maintain corporate control. Empathy respects difference, values opposition, and gives meaning to rebellious behavior.

The parables call upon us to overcome the kinds of impediments regularly faced by those being controlled. In each instance of control from above, Jesus invites his listeners to feel what it is like to be underneath. We must stretch to comprehend. We must work to revive the empathy so completely missing between the characters. How could the tenant farmers possibly believe that their best option is to murder the landlord's son? What makes the younger son so determined to waste his father's inheritance? Listeners who do not share the constraints of these underlings may feel free to criticize them. However, in so doing, they risk failing to see what those who are forced to live within such constraints are trying to achieve.

Empathy

The parables can be understood as exploring the effects of various levels of coercion and the ways in which power over others stifles empathy. The superior who dominates his subordinate subverts himself. He comes to believe in the effectiveness of his coercion. And there is no solution to be found in reversing roles. Just as access to coercion subverts the superior, so also would it subvert the inferior were he to have access to similar power. Coercion leads to conformity in behavior and constriction in speech. It invariably provokes apathy, depression, rage, and rebellion. The greater the coercion the greater the concealment of what is truly going on.

However, we can distinguish between those who manipulate and those who are being manipulated. The former used their power to position themselves out of reach of any influence. We have a greater chance of reaching people who do not have power. Though we do not have to like them, we can enter into their experience in an effort to respect them. Absent respect, the opportunity to discover shared feelings, and hence to facilitate change—both in them and in ourselves—is lost. Respect is the foundation of empathy. It is the essential gateway to positive transformation.

PLACING EMPATHY AT THE CENTER OF OUR CONCEPTION OF GOD

Many people find god language unsatisfying and misleading. This reaction is, in part, a response to centuries of theologians crediting "God" with the power to intervene and make things right. The Christian concept of God also carries with it the freight of Christianity's participation in Western imperialism. In his parables, Jesus says nothing about his God or about God's intervention. Language hinting at God's intervention is first introduced by gospel editors when they imply that the superior figure in the parables acts as God would act.

However, if we reject as wishful thinking any desire to have our God intervene to make things right, we can embrace a God who is profoundly present, persistently luring us to adopt an empathic way of relating that embodies our best self and has the best chance for making things right.

What is the case to be made for placing empathy at the center of our conception of God and at the center of the universe? The human ability to empathize is one of the pinnacles of evolutionary development. It follows on the coalescing of galaxies, the maturing of chemical elements, the emergence of life forms, and the unfolding of self-awareness. All of these

Jesus' Parables Speak to Power and Greed

developments represent extremely complex steps both in ongoing evolution as well as in the human ability to engage life's mysteries.

What of empathy? Because we are so readily impressed by size, we become confused about the importance of things. Galaxies are huge and thus loom large in our awareness. The overwhelming dimensions of lifeless matter, like galaxies, convince us the universe is impersonal. Yet we would (if we could) search across those billions of galaxies, travel among each one's billions of stars, seeking those few planets that might contain some form of life, and those fewer still that might offer the all-important potential for building relationships. For us, the capacity for relating is of greater value than the dispersal of immense amounts of matter across billions of light years of space. How did we come by this fierce desire not to be the only beings, not to be alone? What evolutionary force has moved us towards differentiation, individuation, separation—and then towards relating across our diversity?

At issue is not belief in "God," but whether our god, that is, our individually chosen ultimate concern—the focus of our commitment and dedication—becomes an "it" we imagine we can control, or a "Thou" with whom we can relate. Because of the influence of family culture, this life decision, one of much consequence, usually finds its original essence by the age of eight.

Are we to construe our capacity to feel the feelings of others as uniquely our own? Surely humans cannot be the only beings to possess such an ability, nor should we consider ourselves its originator. Given the fact that humans have achieved this capacity for empathy, it would be unreasonable to imagine that we are the sole possessors of such an exquisitely beautiful aptitude. Rather empathy can be seen as occupying the heart of that force—spread out everywhere across the universe—that we call "God." In secular terms, one translation for God might read, "that presence in the universe that leads to the development of life, to the increasing complexity in life-forms, to the evolution of consciousness, and to the evolution of the ability to empathize."

We need compelling narratives that locate empathy throughout the universe. Such narratives would place our capacity for empathy on par with the delicate balances in the physical universe that fashioned the carbon which, in turn, formed our bodies and led to our self-awareness. Just as the chemical elements so essential to our being exist throughout the universe, so the capacity for empathy so essential to our survival must also emanate from a myriad of far-distant sources. While we should not expect such achievements to have emerged everywhere, we can expect to find them in scattered pinpricks spread out across the magnificent complexity of space. In these locales we can imagine beings who have evolved at least as far as we have, and, in many instances, far beyond.

PLACING EMPATHY AT THE CENTER OF RESOLVING OUR CURRENT MASSIVE MALAISE

At the same time as we acquired the mental facility to engineer our self-destruction, we developed empathy, the singular power essential for our salvation. Although it may seem an insufficient counterbalance to the strongly motivated passion for control, empathy is the one force in the universe able to sustain our survival. What is the case for positioning empathy at the center of the resolution of our current massive malaise?

In creating our God, that is, in identifying what matters most to us, we create our destiny. How then can we understand our God in a way that does not tempt us to invoke God's coercion? If, in Jesus' imagination, his God is yearning for humans to intervene without coercion, how exactly are we to intervene? The answers lie in the discovery that one enters the kingdom of God in a manner similar to how one enters the parables. In our efforts to understand the parables, we are moved to place ourselves inside the experience of both protagonists. The parable requires and rewards such work. Here empathy overcomes the temptation to resort to coercion.

Empathy lies at the heart of Jesus' understanding of the nature of his God. God is with us, yearning, longing, suffering, but always entrusting to us the work of becoming. God can be imagined as that loving force in the universe constantly longing to make just what is unjust. God can be understood as present in whatever articulates and exemplifies how the created order functions best. God can also be apprehended as yearning for us to work together—and as yearning for us to bring them together. One enters the kingdom of God by being with God the way God is with us. Feeling for the other becomes the central resource for understanding the desire of God. It initiates a broad process of listening. In this way of understanding, Jesus' parables may be seen not as promising rescue but rather as inviting us to delve into these stories in the same way God reaches into our world.

We pause at this moment in human history to wonder if, by denigrating a key resource spread throughout the cosmos, we are denying ourselves the chance to avoid self-destruction. Will we use our self-awareness to gain personally and disregard others? Or, by internalizing the pain we might be causing others, will we stop taking and start giving? This is the most promising and most deadly of crossroads.

With increased access to increasingly complex technology, humans are growing in their capacity to understand and evolve, but also to misperceive and contribute to their extinction. Science and religion, each in their own way, can be found on either side of that divide. Science that aspires to plumb the mysteries of the created order can be differentiated from science that misuses control over its workings. Religion searching to discover divine intention can be distinguished from religion preoccupied with the power of divine intervention.

Advances in science have freed us to develop within the limits of observable natural laws. However, science is not positioned to persuade us to accept those limits. By definition the entire skein of forces motivating climate denial falls beyond the reach of scientific authority. Religious sensibility, in concert with the God of the universe, can reinforce our ability to align sensitively with others. We can imagine that the needs of the natural order exist not only within our own awakened feelings for others but also out there among the galaxies. Put differently, sentient individuals who are able to relate to one another will sense that God, or universal evolution, is on their side as they become aware of and adapt to the experience of others. One striking verse in the biblical tradition illustrates such cosmic empathy, "My anguish, my anguish! I writhe in pain! Oh, the walls of my heart! My heart is beating wildly; I cannot keep silent; for I hear the sound of the trumpet, the alarm of war" (Jer 4:19). It is impossible to determine whether the speaker is Jeremiah or God.

We can imagine how God feels towards us as we struggle with climate change. How God feels our rage and disappointment as we see our survival threatened by our fellow humans. How God weeps for us as we destroy our environment. How God rejoices when we live within natural limits. These perceptions can be dismissed as anthropomorphic projections. We create the God we want. However, given that we are dependent on our own experience for conceptualization, this critique applies equally to every single narrative ever conceived to comprehend the essence of reality. But it is still possible to address the problem of bias by evaluating the implications of our choices. Do we privilege the primacy of physical forces over the power of human relations? Are we dazzled by the difference in magnitude between billions of light years and delicate moments of human concern? Do we find that which is subject to the purview of science more persuasive? Most importantly, do we elevate the persuasive power of science over that of religious narrative? (Perhaps nowhere is the inability of science to persuade more evident than in the realm of climate denial.) Whether in religion or elsewhere, we must seek that which has the greatest capacity to impact our growing sense of inadequacy.

In like fashion, the classic criticism made of any effort to diverge from received perspectives about Jesus is that one will find the Jesus one wishes to find. Every conformist, every challenger is subject to this same criticism; no one is free of subjective bias. The reader must therefore make her or his judgment based on the evidence and arguments at hand. When weighing these arguments, the reader should remain alert to the persistent pressure to domesticate radical points of view, that is, to find readings that make fewer demands.

If the parables studied in this book were created by the historical Jesus and the complexities they contain go back to him, what do they tell us about Jesus? They reveal a man who is extraordinarily sensitive to the consequences of domination as it reverberates through society. His narratives provide descriptions of the human situation rather than prescriptions for how that situation should be changed. Jesus was not only a master of the human condition, he was also masterful at drawing people into engaging with it. He does not resolve the difficulties depicted in his parables. In particular, he does not resolve them by having his God intervene. Instead, he trusts his listeners to recognize the issues and then to imagine their resolution. To do so, listeners, too, must change.

The religious imagination is beguiled by concepts of God's omnipotence and omniscience. That emphasis strengthens narratives of divine intervention and weakens narratives of human participation. In contrast, understanding God as the possessor of the most far-reaching and inclusive empathy imaginable can serve as a potent metaphor for how the natural order "desires," "intends for," or "longs for" humans to be and to act.

What God longs for, what Jesus terms "the kingdom or desire of God," might be understood as "human awareness of the ways the created order functions well," e.g., through clean air, clean water, abundant food, healthy bodies, etc., all premised on the collaborative sharing of resources. Human resonance with "God's desire" can then be conceived as involving the capacity to empathize with, and thereby engage with, the needs of fellow humans. The needs of fellow humans, in turn, merge with the requirements of the natural environment (in today's world, most importantly, population control) to support such needs.

Across millennia, humans have vacillated between freeing up resources for others and taking far more than we need for ourselves. Our God, our ultimate concern, can embody a desire to share what we have with others. On the other hand, it can also embody worship of market forces that emphasize helping ourselves. The decision about which inclination we indulge has become pivotal for human survival. Whether or not God exists in the abstract is irrelevant. Far more significant is the nature of the ultimate concern that dominates our day-to-day decision-making. In the briefest terms, are we captivated by "taking hold of" or by "letting be?"

Only the God who longs for us to give to others is represented in the relationships fashioned by Jesus. That aspect of God which mattered most to Jesus, namely, our ability to collaborate with one another, has today become the aspect of God most essential to ongoing human evolution. Choosing a God who is tribal, exclusive, or indifferent, frees us to take whatever we can from others—and thus unencumbers our propensity to destroy our world.

The religious epigram that "God is love" arguably does not represent a sentimental projection but rather a summary of how the universe functions. The human brain can both create and distort relationships in the natural order. At its core, climate denial, which entails the rejection of scientific data, refuses to feel how others, and nature itself, suffer because of our actions. We need to nurture the ability to penetrate such a self-centered dismissal. ("Because I am not hurting, it doesn't matter to me that you are.") We need to enhance our capacity to make visible the hidden experience of victims. ("We are invisible because you refuse to see us.") We need to empower our capability to perceive the pain we inflict on the natural order. ("We—trees, mammals, insects, ocean creatures—are being destroyed because you fail to feel our distress.") This suppressed information is crucial to our survival.

Tribal or corporate self-interest subverts the welfare of the whole. It fragments social relationships into competing groups and thus fails as a survival mechanism. Because God does not intervene to frustrate their purposes, the question of whether God exists is irrelevant to those who insist on more. They are impressed only by power that is obvious. They take the fact that no God opposes them to mean that no opposition exists, that their God reigns supreme.

Empathy

Because it is approaching gradually, they fail to appreciate the threat of climate change. They do not factor its inevitability into their calculation of self-interest. Also missing from that calculation is the reality that, once set in motion, climate change cannot be stopped. It involves all or nothing. Everyone must be on board. For the first time ever, a unified concern for others is the highest form of self-interest.

In the face of impending climate disaster, how can a God who feels for us not intervene to rescue us? Does an empathic God have any chance of countering the human forces that threaten our survival? Our difficulty in imagining an empathic God who permeates the universe arises from our longstanding insistence on an omnipotent God. When we conceive a God who feels our pain, we rush to imagine one who will transform that pain. We look for a God who will fight the Romans, but the God of Jesus suffers with him.

How can a God who feels for us and our survival not also insist on our compliance with the laws of nature? We keep on setting demands and deadlines, whether they be for end-time apocalypses or for the cure of a terminally ill child. When our God does not step in, we conclude that God must be impersonal or, at best, irrelevant. We fail to ponder, for example, the profound intimacy revealed in Jesus' dying cry, "My God, my God, why have you forsaken me?" (Matt 27:46 NRSV). Jesus almost certainly imagined his whole enterprise had failed. What might it be like for his God to stand by, refusing to act, when hearing this cry? What might it be like for God to stand back while feeling our pain? Or while remaining fully with us as we enter into the pain of others?

Jesus' listeners occupy a position vis-à-vis his parable characters that is similar to the one his God occupies towards us. We are simultaneously the providers and the recipients of empathy. As providers, we experience the *inability* to act in that we cannot intervene. As recipients, recognizing that the God of the universe is steadfastly *with* us, we gain the *ability* to act insofar as we can share the experience of the parable characters.

Do we agree with this emphasis on the primacy of personal responsibility? Or do we prefer an all-powerful God who is able to coerce human beings to respond? Does an all-powerful God *want* to coerce the responsiveness of human beings? Or does God's power reside in longing, in yearning—the foundations of respect essential to spark empathy in others? If we conceive of an immensely caring, immanent God, then we are obliged to acknowledge—both in these ancient narratives and in our approach to

Jesus' Parables Speak to Power and Greed

the contemporary world around us—the central role of issues such as love, disappointment, feelings of disrespect and rejection, grief, pain, anger, and concern for the suffering of others. We recognize that the only attitude capable of overcoming this contemporary fracturing of interrelatedness is the ability to imagine what it is like to *be* the other. Most importantly, we come to realize that entering these experiences takes much work and much time.

Never before have we been so pressed for time. We can afford to be patient when observing first-century actors. But today, only a few generations separate us, even the wealthiest among us, from the consequences of our inaction. Reversing the trends that have grown over the course of human history may take more time than we have remaining. Millennia of distortions are now impacting the limits of the earth. They will soon have reached the point where we will have irreversibly destroyed the environment requisite for humans to thrive.

If, as already seems probable, we do not succeed in mitigating the effects of soaring temperatures already locked in place, then we will have tasked future generations with coping with their feelings towards those of us who refused to sacrifice a modicum of prosperity when we could. How will they stomach their bitter disappointment and consuming rage directed at our failure to act? What God has any chance of easing the anger they feel toward earlier generations who so thoroughly and thoughtlessly abandoned them to their fate? Inside this question we can hear God weeping.

Future generations will suffer from our failure. They will have to shoulder the additional burden of restoring empathy for those subgroups who will inevitably go to war with them over increasingly limited resources. They will face an outsized version of the dilemmas our generation has largely avoided. As it did for the Vietnam War, the mantra will become, "Why didn't we put an end to it earlier?" "How could any outcome be worse than that which we now find ourselves facing?"

The response of this book is grounded in Jesus' requirements for penetrating his parables. It involves the centrality of empathy. Jesus places the work of listening at the forefront of his teaching. An abridged version of Matthew's commentary on Jesus' teaching reads as follows,

> [Jesus] told them many things in parables, saying, "Listen . . . listen . . . see . . . perceive . . . hear . . . listen . . . understand . . . listen . . . understand . . . look . . . perceive . . . hear . . . look . . . listen . . . understand . . . see . . . hear." (Matt 13:3–16 NRSV)

Empathy

We begin by acknowledging that empathy is not about us being *with them*. Empathy is first of all about God being *with us*. If we agree that change comes about only through understanding others, we can then ask ourselves whether we want a God who intervenes powerfully or whether we seek a God who shares our suffering. If we choose a suffering God, we will encounter a God who is profoundly with us, one who fully embraces our rage, our hurt, our dashed hopes. "My God, my God, why have you forsaken me?" is not the final word. In our efforts to engage and interact with both the characters in Jesus' parables and with our fellow humans, we are also endeavoring to understand how God is with us. The universe encompasses an unlimited capacity for empathy. The God of the universe longs for us to seek divine presence, to feel in our own suffering God's all-encompassing embrace, and, following Jesus, to trust that God will never forsake us.

Bibliography

Ackerman, Frank. *Can We Afford the Future? The Economics of a Warming World*. London: Zed, 2009.
Baer, Paul, et al. *The Right to Development in a Climate Constrained World: The Greenhouse Development Rights Framework*. Washington, DC: Heinrich Boll Stiftung, 2007.
Bailey, Kenneth E. *Jacob and the Prodigal: How Jesus Retold Israel's Story*. Downers Grove, IL: InterVarsity, 2003.
Banerjee, Neela, et al. "Exxon: The Road Not Taken." *InsideClimate News*, September 16, 2015. insideclimatenews.org/content/Exxon-The-Road-Not-Taken.
Campbell, Joseph. *The Power of Myth*. New York: Anchor, 1991.
Cardinal, Ernesto, ed. *The Gospel in Solentiname*. 4 vols. Translated by Donald Devenish Walsh. Maryknoll, NY: Orbis, 1982.
Climatefiles. "1988 Shell Confidential Report—The Greenhouse Effect." www.climatefiles.com/shell/1988-shell-report-greenhouse/.
———. "1998 Report—Climate Change: What Does Shell Think and Do About It?" www.climatefiles.com/shell/1998-shell-report-think-and-do-about-climate-change/.
Crossan, John Dominic. *God and Empire: Jesus against Rome, Then and Now*. New York: HarperOne, 2007.
Daniel, Will. "U.S. Companies Post Their Biggest Profit Growth in Decades by Jacking up Prices During the Pandemic." *Fortune*, March 31, 2022. Fortune.com/2022/03/31/us-companies-record-profits-2021-price-hikes-inflation/.
Davies, W. D. *The Territorial Dimension of Judaism*. Berkeley: University of California Press, 1982.
de Boer, Martinus C. "Ten Thousand Talents? Matthew's Interpretation and the Redaction of the Parable of the Unforgiving Servant (Matt. 18:23–35)." *Catholic Biblical Quarterly* 50 (1988) 214–32.
Diamond, Jared. *Collapse: How Societies Choose to Fail or Succeed*. New York: Penguin, 2011.
Doukas, Alex. "Talk Is Cheap: How G20 Governments Are Financing Climate Disaster." *OilChange International*, July 5, 2017. Priceofoil.org/2017/07/05/g20-financing-climate-disaster/.
"DuPont vs. the World: Chemical Giant Covered Up Health Risks of Teflon Contamination across Globe." *Democracy Now!*, January 23, 2018. https://www.democracynow.org/2018/1/23/dupont_vs_the_world_chemical_giant.
Ford, Richard Q. *The Parables of Jesus and the Problems of the World*. Eugene, OR: Cascade Books, 2016.

Fortna, Robert T. "Reading Jesus' Parable of the Talents through Underclass Eyes." *Forum* 8.3/4 (1992) 211–28.

Frank, Thomas. *Listen, Liberal: Or, What Ever Happened to the Party of the People?* New York: Metropolitan, 2016.

Funk, Robert W. *Parables and Presence: Forms of the New Testament Tradition.* Philadelphia: Fortress, 1982.

Gambino, Lauren. "'I Love the Poorly Educated': Why White College Graduates Are Deserting Trump." *The Guardian*, October 16, 2016. https://www.theguardian.com/us-news/2016/oct/16/white-college-graduates-donald-trump-support-falling.

Herzog, William R., II. *Parables as Subversive Speech: Jesus as Pedagogue of the Oppressed.* Louisville: Westminster John Knox, 1994.

Hobley, Anthony. "2 Degrees of Separation—Transition Risk for Oil and Gas in a Low Carbon World." *Carbon Tracker*, June 20, 2017. https://www.carbontracker.org/reports/2-degrees-of-separation-transition-risk-for-oil-and-gas-in-a-low-carbon-world-2/.

Hochschild, Arlie Russell. *Strangers in Their Own Land: Anger and Mourning on the American Right.* New York: New Press, 2016.

Isser, Stanley. "The Samaritans and Their Sects." In *The Early Roman Period*, edited by William Horbury et al., 569–78. The Cambridge History of Judaism 3. Cambridge: Cambridge University Press, 1999.

Joyce, Christopher. "Mapping the Potential Economic Effects of Climate Change." *NPR*, June 29, 2017. npr.org/sections/the two-way/2017/06/29/534896130/.

Kähler, Christoph. *Jesu Gleichnesse als Poesie und Therapie.* Wissenschaftliche Untersuchungen zum Neuen Testament 78. Tübingen: Mohr/Siebeck, 1995.

Klein, Naomi. *This Changes Everything: Capitalism vs. the Climate.* New York: Simon & Schuster, 2014.

Kloppenborg, John S. *The Tenants in the Vineyard: Ideology, Economics, and Agrarian Conflict in Jewish Palestine.* Wissenschaftliche Untersuchungen zum Neuen Testament 195. Tübingen: Mohr Siebeck, 2006.

Lawson, Max, and Matthew Martin. "The Commitment to Reducing Inequality Index 2018: A Global Ranking of Governments Based on What They Are Doing to Tackle the Gap between Rich and Poor." *Oxfam International*, October 8, 2018. https://www.oxfam.org/en/research/commitment-reducing-inequality-index-2018.

Makortoff, Kalyeena. "Nearly 94% of Shell Shareholders Reject Emissions Reduction Target in Line with Paris Climate Agreement." *Independent,* May 23, 2017. independent.co.uk/environment/shell-shareholders-94-per-cent-emissions-reduction-target-reject-paris-agreement-climate-change-a7751681.html/.

Mathewes, Charles. "On Self-Deception in Evil—Scholasticism." Disc 6, Lecture 12 of *Why Evil Exists.* Twelve CD lectures issued by the Teaching Company. www.thegreatcourses.com/courses/why-evil-exists.

Mayer, Jane. *Dark Money: The Hidden History of the Billionaires behind the Radical Right.* New York: Anchor, 2017.

McKibben, Bill. "Global Warming's Terrifying New Math: Three Simple Numbers That Add Up to Global Catastrophe—and That Make Clear Who the Real Enemy Is." *Rolling Stone,* July 19, 2012. rollingstone.com/politics/politics-news/global-warmings-terrifying-new-math-188550/.

Bibliography

———. "Winning Slowly Is the Same as Losing." *Rolling Stone*, December 1, 2017. rollingstone.com/politics/politics-news/bill-mckibben-winning-slowly-is-the-same-as-losing-198205/.

Osofsky, Gilbert, ed. *Puttin' on Ole Massa: The Slave Narratives of Henry Bibb, William Wells Brown, and Solomon Northup*. New York: Harper & Row, 1969.

Reilly, Katie. "Read Hillary Clinton's 'Basket of Deplorables' Remarks about Donald Trump Supporters." *Time*, September 10, 2016. https://time.com/4486502/hillary-clinton-basket-of-deplorables-transcript/.

Rohrbaugh, Richard L. "A Peasant Reading of the Parable of the Talents/Pounds: A Text of Terror?" *Biblical Theology Bulletin* 23 (1993) 32–39.

Toynbee, Arnold J. *A Study of History*. Oxford: Oxford University Press, 1946.

wa Thiong'o, Ngũgĩ. *Devil on the Cross*. African Writers Series 200. London: Heinemann, 1982.

Watts, Jonathan. "We Have 12 Years to Limit Climate Change Catastrophe, Warns UN." *The Guardian,* October 8, 2018. theguardian.com/environment/2018/oct/08/global-warming-must-not-exceed-15c-warns-landmark-un-report/.

Yourcenar, Marguerite. *Memoirs of Hadrian*. Translated by Grace Frick with the author. New York: Farrar, Straus & Giroux, 2005.

www.ingramcontent.com/pod-product-compliance
Lightning Source LLC
Chambersburg PA
CBHW030859170426

43193CB00009BA/664